Making Rainbows

Making Rainbows

What Are Life and Life After Death All About

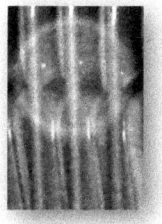

Prudence Ann Smith MD

Copyright © 2015 Prudence Ann Smith MD
All rights reserved.

ISBN-13: 9780692560327
ISBN-10: 0692560327
Library of Congress Control Number: 2015917516
Belle Publishers, Tulare, CA

Forward

MAKING RAINBOWS – what are life and life after death all about? Ever go through a review of your life or a self-assessment? I think it's something you do as you get older, when you face your own mortality, and ask those questions, "Who am I, what is the purpose of life, what have I learned from it, and how have I dealt with the loss of loved ones and my own inevitable death?

I am a baby boomer and I have been doing a self-evaluation, addressing those questions and these are my answers. I may not understand everything, but this is my attempt to make sense of life's biggest questions and greatest mysteries.

Information in this book that has been channeled is indented. Other comments inspired by Spirit are designated as such. Some commentary consists of my own personal observations and conclusions drawn from my experiences. As such, these are opinions, given in hope that they may comfort, enlighten, or inspire.

As in all instances in life, if something resonates with you, I hope that if may be of benefit, but if not, discard it, as we all must arrive at our own ultimate truth on our journeys.

Dedication

To my everlasting love, my guide,

And my beloved dogs, Holly, Angel, Dancer, Noel, Belle, and Jingles

All the yearnings in my heart have come out and become the love I have with you.

I am now free to be and not just sing.

I lived within my imagination and hopes and now my hopes are realized.

The living is better than the dreaming.

My desires have come true and I no longer have only to live in my thoughts and fancies

But live in my truth, which is the present fulfillment of all my deepest wishes and desires.

My dream is no longer merely a dream but walks with me, talks with me and kisses me goodnight, for as the poet said, it truly is now a good night.

The love between us is one and is the past, the present, and future. All that I could ever hope for I now live, the love and togetherness we share. My longing is fulfilled and my life is complete.

To my beloved, my love everlasting, writing on the script of eternity.

To be with you is indeed Heaven to me.

I have the courage to be who I am, without the different faces presented to please others.

I leave behind the hurt, the pain, and the loss. I have you forever.

I am content and my soul has peace at last.

To my Guide, my Loved One

Sometimes I am your child. Sometimes I am your mother. Sometimes I am your wife. Sometimes I am your husband. Sometimes I am your friend. But I am your partner always.

Table of Contents

Chapter 1	Advice	1
Chapter 2	Animals: What I Learned from my Dogs	5
Chapter 3	Miscellaneous Observations	10
Chapter 4	Afterlife – Similarities and Differences	28
Chapter 5	The Effectual Power of Belief	31
Chapter 6	Spirit Body	32
Chapter 7	Bonds	40
Chapter 8	Spiritual Change	44
Chapter 9	Choices	53
Chapter 10	Cold Spots	55
Chapter 11	Commitments	57
Chapter 12	Communication with the Other Side	60
Chapter 13	Compatibility	64
Chapter 14	Contradictions	67
Chapter 15	Spirit Counsel	69
Chapter 16	Diversity	71
Chapter 17	Forgiveness	73
Chapter 18	Fulfilling Dreams	76
Chapter 19	Dying	78
Chapter 20	Energy and Einstein's Equation	79
Chapter 21	Afterlife Environment	81
Chapter 22	Experience, Life's Best Teacher	83

Chapter 23	Feelings and the Bigger Picture	85
Chapter 24	Moving Forward	86
Chapter 25	Maintaining Individual Freedom	87
Chapter 26	Spirit Gender	90
Chapter 27	God and Related Philosophical Topics	94
Chapter 28	Mediums and Grief	104
Chapter 29	Guides	106
Chapter 30	Habits	108
Chapter 31	Healing	110
Chapter 32	Humor on the Other Side	113
Chapter 33	Identity	115
Chapter 34	Other Dimension Incarnations	120
Chapter 35	Maintaining Integrity	121
Chapter 36	Learning From Life	122
Chapter 37	The Lesson	124
Chapter 38	Life Lessons	128
Chapter 39	The Purpose of Life	130
Chapter 40	Spirit Life	132
Chapter 41	Loss and Karma	139
Chapter 42	A Love Story	142
Chapter 43	Spirit Manifestations- Hallucination or Reality	145
Chapter 44	Love and True Marriage	147
Chapter 45	The Real Me	149
Chapter 46	Finding Meaning	152
Chapter 47	The Medium – Spirit Connection	154
Chapter 48	Accuracy in Mediumship	156
Chapter 49	Mediumship	159
Chapter 50	Memorable Messages	173
Chapter 51	Planning Mistakes	177
Chapter 52	Near Death Experiences	180
Chapter 53	Negative Levels – Punishment?	184

Chapter 54	Plans For Negativity	189
Chapter 55	Spiritual Oneness	190
Chapter 56	Other Comments	191
Chapter 57	Experiencing the Paranormal	194
Chapter 58	Letting Go of the Past	195
Chapter 59	What Are Our Paths?	197
Chapter 60	Retention of Personality	199
Chapter 61	Planes	200
Chapter 62	Personal Preference and the Law of Like Attraction	202
Chapter 63	Pretensions	205
Chapter 64	Addressing Problems	206
Chapter 65	Personal Proof	208
Chapter 66	God Given Purpose	210
Chapter 67	Making Rainbows	212
Chapter 68	Communication – Readings From Living People	215
Chapter 69	Spirit Recognition	216
Chapter 70	Reincarnation Choices	221
Chapter 71	Negative Past Relationships	223
Chapter 72	Relationships	225
Chapter 73	Selfishness	243
Chapter 74	Sex	244
Chapter 75	Spirit Sight	245
Chapter 76	Spirit Sightings By Humans	248
Chapter 77	Trance Channeling	251
Chapter 78	A Song	263
Chapter 79	Current Theories	266
Chapter 80	Spirit Thought Transmission	269
Chapter 81	Trust	270
Chapter 82	Seeking The Truth	272

Chapter 83	Twin Flames	275
Chapter 84	Veil Between the Worlds	277
Chapter 85	Verbal Abuse	278
Chapter 86	Near Death Visions	279
Chapter 87	Destiny and Free Will	282
Chapter 88	Words of Comfort	283
Chapter 89	The Physical World	285
Chapter 90	Afterthoughts	288
	Bibliography	291
	Author Biography	293

1

Advice

There are many sayings about advice. One of them is, "Good advice, good advice, it costs you nothing and it's worth the price."

Many, as they grow older, begin to reflect on their lives. I thought, what could I tell someone that would be of value? Certainly I must have gained some insight or wisdom from my busy and tumultuous life. I've had many ups and downs, a lot of accomplishments and failures.

I've looked back at my life and thought, what would I have done if I had to live my life over? What would I have changed? What have I learned from what I endured? What would I do to make my life happier or better? How could I have avoided the mistakes I made? What did I learn that would enable me to produce better results?

I realized that some things I couldn't have changed, just because I can only control my own actions, but not all of the circumstances of life that I was born into and encountered. I couldn't control what other people said and did, only my own reactions to them. Many of the larger things in society and the world we have little impact on as individuals, such as racism, injustice, poverty, and crime. Many circumstances are dictated by chance and outside of our control.

It has been said that before we came to this world we planned the events and circumstances we would encounter to learn from them. I certainly have learned from mine, both the good and the bad. If I were given the opportunity to relive my life, there are many different choices I would have made. I guess that's good when we can say that, because it means we've learned something.

I learned that in many situations, we have the answer in us, but we don't always listen. Paying attention to what people do, not just what they say, helps us to read between the lines. Wisdom comes from experience. Do you recall the saying, "Fool me once, shame on you, fool me twice, shame on me?" Paying attention, testing the waters, reading the signs, thinking with your head as well as your heart, will help you avoid much heartache.

Finding out the truth can be difficult. How many people have gotten involved with a situation or person and found out later it wasn't what they thought it was, or, if it was, that it changed into something else down the line? How can you tell what someone really means or thinks? You can't, always. Not all mistakes can be avoided, but developing our spiritual antennas is certainly a help. In certain cases, we need to set our SPAM filters higher, be more sensitive or cautious, and perhaps avoid some of the unscrupulous characters before they can do their damage. Awareness often comes at a great price.

I always try to work on making more informed choices.

Another issue we need to address is what makes us happy. That answer is unique to each of us. What is right for one may not be for another. Sometimes something or someone we think will make us happy doesn't. It may be material possessions, a home, a career, fame, a partner, or a creative pursuit. Part of the learning process is discovering what is truly important for us.

I found my answer. Having a comfortable, safe home, a fulfilling career, an interesting and absorbing hobby, are all worthy and have merit. But the most important thing in the world for me is love – sharing a deep, reciprocal bond with a compatible, loving companion. Sharing love and support with a family is paramount. Certainly, whatever we accomplish in this world in terms of good or bad, influencing the lives of others, is the legacy we leave behind us. All that we take with us to the other side when we cross over is the lessons we have learned and the love we have.

I can't imagine a world without love, and wouldn't want to live in one. No amount of wealth, possessions, or accomplishments can make up for a lack of love. There would be a great, empty hole in my life without it. All of the other positive aspects of life are good, but that one is the most essential to my happiness.

What else have I learned? To the best of my ability to do good, to try to treat others as I wish to be treated, to act with kindness and empathy, to practice love and forgiveness, to promote mercy and justice. Strengthen fortitude to do good and resist temptation. Share knowledge. Inspire hearts. Spread the truth. The greatest truth is love.

PRUDENCE ANN SMITH MD

A poem for my loved one and guide:

> Devotion
> Your warmth is my jewel,
> Your love is my treasure,
> It's wealth beyond words
> And joy beyond measure;
> My devotion is yours
> And it will extend
> Like my love, without limits
> For time without end.

2

Animals: What I Learned from my Dogs

WHAT I LEARNED from Belle:

Belle was the runt of the litter and she always put a smile on my face. She had a lot of physical illness in her lifetime and I felt honored and privileged to be her caregiver.

She was very intelligent and understood a wide vocabulary, sometimes almost with an uncanny perception. She was also very loyal and I bonded with her very strongly during one crisis in which I almost lost her. She did do something once that some would consider "naughty" but nothing could interrupt my love for her. She truly was my child with four legs and a tail.

From Belle I learned unconditional love.

What I learned from Holly:

Holly came along when Belle died. I felt no one could replace Belle or the love I had for her. She and I almost had a telepathic bond. Holly was different. Holly wasn't as quick to understand or as forward or cuddly. She wasn't as quick to seek out attention. But Holly was a lover. She was a sweetheart and didn't have a mean bone in her body. No, she didn't replace Belle's love, but I loved her just as much in a different way. I would have given her the same care and miss that always-accepting, innocent sweetness, and that special love she gave and had for all. I learned that one love doesn't replace another, but can be just as strong in a different way. I miss her just as much as I missed Belle, and learned that one love can be as cherished as another, although different.

From Holly I learned that no one can ever replace anyone else, but there can be many loves, equally important, but different.

The British spiritualists deny the continuation of animals after death, stating that they do not have souls.

I have accumulated much evidence that animals do live on in the afterlife.

The first medium I ever consulted, Jeffrey Wands, author of "Another Door Opens", said I had two dogs in spirit and that one was with my mother. This was true. The reading was conducted by telephone, and he had never met or known me. I never asked him about nor mentioned animals.

Harvey, my friend and colleague, gave a reading to a woman at a JamesVan Praagh seminar stating, "The dog isn't in spirit yet." This would indicate that when dogs pass, they continue in spirit. When Harvey gave that reading, he said he didn't know where that term came from, "in spirit", but that the words were given to him. He heard them.

A medium from Holland named Klassina brought through my former dog Belle, and showed something with her nose, scrunching it, which was when I kissed her, which I frequently did.

I have a friend who is a medium and uses the pseudonym Karuna. Karuna's animals, including a gecko and a monkey, came through at a Robert Brown seminar in Virginia Beach. These are not typical pets that most people have, and the medium, A. J. Barrera, brought them through.

Harvey brought Karuna's cat through not long after it had passed.

D., at an Austyn Wells seminar, brought my two dogs through, with extensive evidential detail, completely and accurately, while she did a "blindfolded" reading, and described everything precisely, thinking these were two human children.

Hollister Rand brings animals through regularly.

Karuna brought my dog, Holly, through shortly after she died, and let me know she was safe and being cared for by a loved one. The reading incorporated my loved one's sense of humor. Karuna saw him dressed in a black and white tuxedo with a top hat and fake moustache, and my dog, Holly, was also dressed in a black and white bib with a black top hat and a fake moustache, both performing a dance routine together. This was very evidential for me because it reflected my loved one's sense of humor. It gave me great comfort to know she was received by others and at his side.

A new medium, also at Hollister Rand's recent seminar, who stated she had never experienced clairvoyance, brought through one image after another, like a collage of my life, referring to a small black dog, my first dog, Jingles, a small brown dog associated with Christmas and Minnesota, who was my red beagle, Belle, whom I had received as a Christmas present while I was living in Minnesota, and a dog with a red collar, who was my recently passed dog Holly, whose red collar is now hanging on the deer horns from my father in my home.

In that same seminar given by Hollister Rand, the medium, D. said, "----- ", your husband and guide, says he's not just the gatekeeper, he's the dogkeeper.

At this same seminar, a participant medium, N., took pictures of us, and an orb showed up next to my face with a perfect replica of my recently passed dog, Holly's face in it. In addition I set the intention, and another photograph showed three orbs, one of my passed loved one and partner, another of a dog, and one that she described as angelic.

Matthew Smith, a British spiritualist and tutor at the Arthur Findlay College of Mediumship, had a spirit formerly named Albert speak through him while in trance and refer to the horse he had when he lived during the period of Queen Victoria's reign, and said the horse, Alice, which he had loved, was still with him on the other side.

There are those who feel that dogs don't have souls, that they don't go to Heaven, and that we never see them again. I am glad I am not one of those people. For those animal lovers who have lost their beloved pets, I have received substantial evidence that our animals continue living on the other side and that they will meet us when we join them on the rainbow bridge.

A picture of me with my dog, Holly's, orb next to my head. The picture was taken and reviewed in my presence and is not fabricated.

MAKING RAINBOWS

My dog, Holly

3

Miscellaneous Observations

Various insights I have gained from my guide, from readings, both given and received, and corroborated in the literature at large, are as follows:

Regarding soulmates

Soulmates are members of our soul group in the afterlife. They are souls we have interacted with in various relationships, including romantic, familial, and fraternal, from multiple lifetimes. There is an eternal connection or link between soul group members, who interact for the purpose of giving or receiving lessons that provide for soul growth.

As such, relationships may be anywhere along the spectrum from idyllic to negative and difficult. Soulmates with whom we have particularly close bonds and harmony may act as our guardian angels on the other side. Often, an unexplainable, intense attraction to or rapport with someone can be present with soulmates.

Think of those in your life that you feel instantly at home with, who resonate with you, and with whom you feel a "magnetic" draw. These are often your soulmates.

Our connection with our soulmates is eternal, which can explain the devastating feelings of incompletion and irreparable loss when a soulmate dies. It can even feel as though a part of us has died with them. If one partner dies, he or she can remain a partner to the living one, both choosing to move forward together. The one who is deceased can choose to act as a guardian angel to the other. That means the deceased partner opts to remain near and help the living one, waiting for their arrival on the other side, rather than moving on and separating. Both the living and deceased partners each have one foot in each world, always remaining present with one another.

Among the closest of soulmates, there can even be unions proclaimed between the two, to remain with one another throughout eternity. Love is eternal and, we, as souls, are eternal, so love never dies. Such unions represent an eternal bond, an intertwining or union of souls. When two souls have such a connection, they are always together, whether in the physical world, the spiritual world, or both.

My loved one in spirit has given the infinity sign to mediums in readings for me, symbolizing our endless bond. He has also communicated to several mediums that we are twin flames, the closest of soulmate relationships.

When one person feels an intense emotional connection with another person, even if they have not had much experience together in the physical world, they are likely feeling a soul connection from the other side.

* * *

Regarding the roles we play

I have said to my loved one, distinctions are artificial. They reflect roles we play from time to time. Sometimes I am (act as) your child. Sometimes I am your mother. Sometimes I am your wife. Sometimes I am your husband. Sometimes I am your friend. But I am your partner always.

* * *

Regarding spirit reunions

Our loved ones may be there to greet us when we cross over to the other side. It is a happy celebration. My cousin indicated from the spirit world that she was happy to reunite with those she loved, and had missed those who had gone on before her in her later years. My loved one, soul partner, and guide has indicated he will remain with me until it is my time to cross over, and will then be there to receive me and accompany me to the other side.

* * *

Regarding the time of our death

The time and manner of our death has been determined by us in the afterlife before we were born. I understand that, within bounds, based upon our actions, we can to a degree hasten or postpone that time. This does not preclude some accidental events, which can usher us to the afterlife before the preplanned time, as we all have free will.

MAKING RAINBOWS

When our soul has completed its job or purpose in life, it leaves. The absence of a will to live can also affect the time of our departure. A now deceased relative of mine used to say that you will pass when it's your time, and, to a large extent, this appears to be true. Our departure is most often a part of our pre-designated path, but also can be from a random accident or act of violence.

Sometimes souls can fine-tune the moment of their departure, waiting for someone to arrive, waiting for a specific time for purposes of obtaining closure, or waiting for someone to leave so that the other person does not have to witness the death.

When my mother passed away on a ventilator in the ICU when I was a medical student, it was after I received a sign from her that she could hear me. She was in a coma-like state but was finally able to communicate her awareness of my presence and what I said to her by wiggling her toes. This was emotionally and psychologically important to me, and as she went into renal failure the next day and had to be removed from the ventilator, as a budding medical professional, I then knew that the medical circumstances were such that she would not "turn the corner", and that her situation was terminal.

The events and timing were so "coincidental", that I have since realized that she had hung on to enable me to prepare myself, had let me know she could hear me, and was able to align her departure at a time when I knew nothing else could be done, that her death was inevitable, and I would not have to live with guilt. That was when I was able to let go. After that, my mother made her transition.

* * *

Regarding rebirth

We choose our birth location and parents in conjunction with our soul group for the purpose of mutual learning. When there is a miscarriage, a soul may have chosen not to incarnate due to a change of plans, or the timing of the incarnation may not have been appropriate.

* * *

Regarding paths

Our path is the reason we came to earth in the first place. Paths may involve teaching lessons through relationships and life situations. They are our preplanned course, almost like an obstacle course in Boot Camp, designed to teach ourselves and others lessons.

The path involves a general direction and circumstances, but we determine how we will react to those relationships and situations with free will. We can alter our path while we are alive, so it is not written in stone. But if we do, we will encounter other challenges.

Many times people blame themselves after the loss of a loved one for not doing more to prevent a death or to change the outcome. Sometimes those challenges and obstacles were meant to be encountered, and were fore-written into your loved one's path. We cannot protect our loved ones from all difficulties or prevent all tragedies. Our loved one has their own path, which we cannot always change, as they have free will, and those difficulties are a part of their path.

Sometimes early deaths are a part of that path and cannot be prevented. Often a soul is required to leave even when the human mind doesn't want to. Some paths include mental or physical handicaps to teach others patience and compassion. I have a relative with such a handicap, and received a message from her mother on the other side that she will no longer have any deficits when she crosses over.

One medium, Lisa Williams, said that wherever you are right now is where you were meant to be. Another medium, Austyn Wells, said that when we encounter negative circumstances, we should always ask "Why did this happen for me?" In other words, what are we meant to learn from the situation? How are we meant to endure or overcome it? What does this teach us about ourselves? How can we best address it or cope with it?

We do not have control of all the experiences we encounter in our lives or the lives of our loved ones. We each have free will in how we respond to and address those issues. I was told from spirit that my loved one followed his path to the end, and I am following mine.

It is difficult for a "control freak" like myself to come to terms with the fact that the only thing I can determine is my own choices and actions, not the entire course of my life, much less that of the world. Shanna Spalding St. Clair's book, "Karma I and II", states that our mission is to make better choices from among the alternatives offered to us. We can't always fix everything for ourselves or anyone else. Our lives are destiny intermingled with free will, enabling us to steer the course of destiny to a degree.

At a mediumship seminar given by Austyn Wells, my cohort, Harvey, gave a profound message from spirit to one of the sitters he was reading for. The message was, "Conflict is the path to resolution and the way to enlightenment." In other words, conflict is a natural part of the life process and shouldn't be regarded as all negative. Without conflict we would never learn how to overcome obstacles, make better choices, or heal relationships. It is what we do when we are faced with conflict or tough decisions that really counts. Having to address it isn't easy, but learning to make choices that are in the best interest of ourselves and all involved is a blessing in disguise. Coping with tragedy, pain, loss, and contentions makes us stronger. Making the best of a bad situation is an invaluable asset. That is how we attain contentment and happiness.

Have you ever heard the old expression, "That's what separates the men from the boys"? Learning coping mechanisms, making wise choices, and finding resolutions are a part of our soul growth.

That doesn't mean we can "fix" everything with our correct decisions, because others have free will and can choose to react as they wish, with their own decisions. We will continue to have problems and pain as long as we are in the physical body, but we are learning to make the best choices possible, to maximize the good we do, to better our condition as much as possible, and to incorporate what our spirit knows into our physical reality. When we return to the other side it will be easy to see what we were supposed to learn. But I believe that what we choose to do with what we have, the hand we are dealt, is important, and that the wisdom we gain will make our lives better and happier, both upon this side of the "veil" and the other. In the words of Shakespeare, "All's well that ends well."

One would think that psychics or mediums, who are attuned to and in connection with the other side, would lead charmed lives. Others may think mediums have an inside track, advice or forewarnings from their loved ones, that they might be able to avoid errors or sidestep misfortunes and tragedies in life. This is patently false. First of all, mediums are human like all others and have their own human weaknesses, make their own human mistakes. No one is perfect. Second, if they were spared all mishaps and problems by their loved ones and guides, they would escape their purpose for being in the world in the first place. They wouldn't learn the lessons if they cheated and got all the answers to the test. As human beings, we're all in the same boat, and sometimes its sink or swim.

Several mediums I know lost their children. One has recently had a child in critical condition in the hospital. Another has a problematic marriage and several are divorced. Yet another just broke up with her partner and is having severe financial issues. And one, with a chronic disease herself, has to work and care for her husband, who is gravely ill. My good friend, the medium, Karuna, put it this way when I was discussing this subject with her. "Mediums are not exempt from the fragilities of life."

I was told by my guides, "Everything works out as it is meant to, including our circumstances and the repercussions of our decisions, for our learning and our ultimate betterment as souls."

* * *

Regarding mistakes

I have a relative who used to make me laugh with a crazy old saying, "Everyone's crazy but me and thee, and I'm not too sure about thee." Well, at times, I'm not too sure about me, either. I've made my share of mistakes in life. Who hasn't? The proverb in the Bible about the woman caught in adultery states, "Let him who is without sin cast the first stone," and all turned and walked away. I've never met anyone perfect. In fact, in the Bible, Jesus had said none are perfect except for the Father, and He is in heaven. Whether or not you subscribe to an organized religion, the point is universal. We wouldn't need to be here if we were perfect.

But what do those in spirit think of our mistakes? All of the answers I, myself, have gotten from those on the other side and through other mediums indicate that spirits have empathy and withhold judgment. When they undergo the Life Review and see their own mistakes, they become more sensitive and tolerant of those of others. One spirit said they each honor the best part of each other. Another said we shouldn't look upon them as mistakes, but as lessons learned. One spirit, coming through another medium, gave me a comical image of us with cows' heads, meaning we can be obtuse when we wrong others. My mother, communicating from the spirit world, said that the irritations and conflicts between people become little hills rather than big mountains. Certainly, people maintain their differences of opinion and individual preferences and characteristics, but become more understanding when they can see their own faults.

After all, we are all works in progress. My guide put it succinctly when he said about a living relative with whom one of the sitters had a problematic relationship, "He is unaware, uninformed." Regarding my own erroneous ways of thinking and regretted actions, my guide said to me, "You weren't evil. You were misguided." Those in spirit can identify with us and are supportive rather than critical when we are hard upon ourselves for the mistakes we have made. They provide us with encouragement, inspiration, and support when we want to change for the better.

* * *

Regarding grief, regrets, and the past

Grief is natural when someone departs physically – even for mediums, who know there is continuing life. Oftentimes a painful loss is the impetus for someone opening up to the other side through their mediumship. I, myself, and several friends who lost children, entered on the path to mediumship through profound grief.

Grief, although a catalyst for the development of spiritual abilities and communication, is a double-edged sword, as it also renders communication more difficult. It lowers our vibration as do all things negative, making it more difficult for our loved ones on the other side to lower their vibration to communicate. Grief and depression make it more difficult for those we love to get through to us.

Emotion is particularly difficult for mediums when they connect with their own departed loved ones, making it more difficult to receive information objectively. When you are emotionally involved it is difficult to get an unbiased message and get your own mind out of the way.

Regrets about how we handled something in the past, the "woulda, coulda, shoulda", are only helpful in allowing us to determine what we should have done and how we would react if we were to encounter the situation again. Overbearing remorse can paralyze us and prevent our forward progression. We must actively seek out our mistakes and use them to light our path to better decisions in the future, turning something negative into something positive. We can't change what we've done, but we can change what we're going to do.

* * *

Regarding spirit awareness

Spirits are aware of what is happening in our lives, and often help us from behind the scenes. They inspire us to better choices if we listen, and our choices and actions can also be a teaching template for those on the other side to see how we handle something that might have been a stumbling block for them.

We are all interwoven into a tapestry, each affecting the other lives we encounter, as well as our own. That is how we change, and the things we all say and do have a ripple effect on others' lives. That is our greatest legacy to one another – to change another's life for the better, by word or by example. One spirit referred to it as a complex dance that we all do with one another, each affecting and changing the others' lives.

There is a mutual "telephone" line of communication if we are open and sensitive to it. Some who are sensitive can see, hear, or feel spirits. Likewise, spirits can hear what we think, feel what we feel, sense what we sense, and see what we see. In the spirit world there are no secrets, no deception, no false pretenses.

If there were masks that we wore in our lifetime, they come off on the other side, and we are known for who we truly are.

* * *

MAKING RAINBOWS

Regarding resolving issues

Spirits encourage us to resolve conflicts and issues while we are alive. Otherwise those problems follow us to the other side and must be resolved there. Albert, channeled by Matthew Smith, an Arthur Findlay college tutor and medium, said he had to "put it right" when he got to the other side. My cousin, Barbie, stated that our issues can bleed over to the other side and some drama can remain. It's best to go over with a clean slate to the best of our ability. Otherwise we pick up where we left off and it's much better to release the baggage and travel light.

When we experience guilt, we must be able to forgive ourselves as well as asking our loved ones for forgiveness. If they can forgive us, why can't we forgive ourselves? If we can forgive others that have harmed us when they ask for forgiveness, we should be able to give ourselves permission to forgive ourselves as well.

When we regret something we've done, we must eventually move past it, rather than being on a continual treadmill of remorse over the past. Otherwise, while we are looking out the rearview mirror, we may miss the positive chances we have for the future and let the past destroy the happiness we could have down the line.

An old saying says that time waits for no man. Don't let past mistakes destroy your future. Then you have effectively made two mistakes instead of one.

Regarding the power of positive thinking

All thoughts are energy and have power. Fears and worries can draw negative experience to us, just as positive thoughts can help produce positive results. Remember GIGO, garbage in, garbage out? If we expect or dwell too much on the negative, we create negative results. If we cultivate positive thoughts, we produce positive results. What we plant, we yield. It is important to control our thoughts, as they direct our actions and subsequently our future.

Medium Kim Russo, on the series "The Haunting Of", explains on the episode with actor Johnathon Schaech, that when we realize we have made a mistake, we should proceed to change our lives in faith, not in fear.

There is one caveat to this advice. That is that if some calamity, something negative is a part of our path, then no amount of positive thinking or hope will be able to circumvent it. In certain cases negative things are meant to happen for our learning.

* * *

Regarding suicide

Those who take themselves over are not condemned. They require healing for the pain that led to their decision. Understanding the hopelessness one feels in that situation, they can help others with despair similar to theirs, and can become helpers or teachers for others who find life's events overwhelming.

MAKING RAINBOWS

When I was in a particularly down mood one day, I got a reading from Sharon Harvey, an Arthur Findlay college of mediumship tutor, on the radio one Saturday. Low and behold, who should come through but my dear friend's son, W., who gave me encouragement. He had crossed himself over and is sensitive to the problem of depression, now helping others who undergo that same problem to the best of his ability.

* * *

Regarding synchronicities

Coincidences are often not coincidental. Many so-called coincidences are messages from spirit, or things that are meant to happen. There is a larger plan which we cannot see with earthly eyes, a greater design. Many things which seem accidental are actually part of that plan.

Looking at my life as I do now, I believe that I was meant to lose my loved one, and as a consequence, open up to spirit and change my life. I no longer think it a coincidence that I was born into a family with a medium for a grandmother. I no longer think it an accident of timing that I changed my life when I rediscovered my loved one in spirit. Everything fell into place at the right time.

If we knew everything while on the earth, we wouldn't make mistakes and learn lessons. I believe that everything happens for a reason, even though we may not comprehend it at the time. I now believe in a greater design, that, even with the foibles and pain of living, is for our eventual betterment, and ultimately for our good. Certainly, the evil in life is not good, but I believe in a divine purpose and restitution, and that ultimately our suffering is rewarded with joy.

Often a tragedy changes us for the better. Many soul contracts are planned with a loss in mind that will nudge others to find a deep reserve of inner strength, leading them to go outside of themselves to help others in pain and grief. Sometimes the most painful events change us the most, and direct us to a better path.

If something has made you more tolerant, more forgiving, more helpful, more charitable, more loving, or more compassionate, it's likely that "that something" was planned or meant to change lives. This is the greater purpose that we have to discern through the pain – those things which catapult us into better action. It is difficult to see the bigger picture through eyes that are clouded by the physical vesture, and only looking through the eyes of spirit can give us glimpses of that better joy, hope, and life that awaits us.

Even on a day to day level, some things which seem coincidental actually aren't. To give an example, my friend Karuna, who is a medium, has more than once had her music on her Ipad begin playing in the middle of a song on its own when she was using the GPS for driving directions and not even touching the device. The songs that played by themselves contained lyrics that were meaningful to her current situation, and another was a song played at her mother's funeral.

Another male acquaintance, P., who is a medium, turned the car radio on to the song, "You'll Be There", by George Strait, which contains the lyric, "I'll see you on the other side", when he was in deep grief over the loss of his wife.

If we attune ourselves to the world around us, we see that many so-called coincidences contain messages for us from those we love on the other side.

* * *

Regarding maintaining connection

When we think lovingly of those we have lost, look at pictures of them, do things they liked or are reminiscent of them, they are closer to us. Positive things should enhance our connection. If we think about them, they know what we are thinking. They know our thoughts, feelings, and deepest emotions. If we sit down and write them a letter, they will know what we have written.

The connection is never broken, it is only unapparent to many of us while in the physical body.

* * *

Regarding spirit contact

My loved one has made his presence known to me by words, electronic manifestations, and touch. An interesting phenomenon recently occurred. I have felt my loved one's touch before, sometimes as a palpable energy, moving my arm or touching my skin, other times as a tingling energy or jolt of electricity.

But this time was unexpected. I had been eating an orange and my hands were wet with the juice. I suddenly felt my loved one's energy in my left hand, and it felt "solid", touchable, like his physical hand. It was a real sensation and I almost couldn't believe it. Afterward I pondered, what would have made the difference. I realized that acidic liquids are good conductors of electricity, and I think that the orange juice coating the surface of my hand enabled me to feel his "electromagnetic touch" so intensely.

* * *

Regarding suffering and healing

We all have our share of suffering in this life. None of us escapes unscathed. The grass may look greener on the other side of the fence, but often it isn't. When you look through the magnifying glass, often that perfect life isn't perfect. There are many different types of troubles – relationship, financial, career, health, substance abuse, lies, infidelity, to name a few.

Suffering can lead to healing. All of us need to heal over something. I understand that much healing from the losses and traumas of the world occurs on the other side. Seeing the bigger picture may help us to understand our pain and the reason for it, but does not ameliorate the pain. That is why we all need and benefit from healing, either in this world or the next.

* * *

Regarding prayer

One of the people on the television series, "Project Afterlife", returned from a near death experience to say that he had seen prayers as energy, as jets of light shooting toward God. The medium, Vanora St. Clair, said that her family in the afterlife has contacted her, saying that her choice of a spiritual pathway has had a positive effect upon the whole family and soul group. Even those on the other side benefit from prayer, saying that it moves them forward and lifts them up. Prayer evidently has an effect not only on those of us in the physical, but upon our loved ones in spirit as well.

MAKING RAINBOWS

Whether in spirit or in body, we are all energy. Prayers are energy and affect the spirit, elevating the spirit vibration, promoting healing, and helping the spirit to progress.

* * *

Regarding infinite possibilities

A woman on the show, "Project Afterlife", who had a near death experience, returned to say that in the afterlife, nothing is impossible. There are no limits. All of our positive desires and dreams can come true.

I have been told that the desires of our hearts, if not harmful to others, can be fulfilled. One of my relatives said, if we really knew what the afterlife was like, we might be standing in line to jump off a cliff. Of course, he was kidding, but he has since contacted me from the other side through a medium, and when I asked him, is the afterlife as wonderful as we imagined, his answer was, "Even better."

4

Afterlife – Similarities and Differences

IN WHAT WAYS is the afterlife like the earth life we know, and in what ways is it different?

My Guide:

It is not materially or physically based. Physical objects are not needed, such as food, furniture, and buildings.

Patterns are not restrictive. No work is needed to maintain physical form. Punishments for crimes are not needed. Childbearing and child-rearing labors are not needed. Hospitals to care for the physical body are not needed.

It is a mental reality.

We are liberated from physical constraints and limitations that are necessities for maintenance of the physical form.

We do retain a conscious mind, identity, and emotions that can interact with others without the physical constraints and obligations.

We can re-create the physical enjoyments, but the conditions of the afterlife are as advanced as television would be to a cave man. Other enjoyments, visual, auditory, emotional, as well as feelings, learning, and ideas, are all available, but less structured, less constrained.

Harvey's guides:

What aspects of the afterlife are similar to earth life, and what aspects are different?

Characteristics of the lower levels of the afterlife are very familiar and similar to what we know on earth. We can hang onto familiar things and then drop them and be someplace else.

One of the differences is time travel. There is no time or space as we know it on the other side. Time and space are endless. The spirit continually evolves.

What we can perceive is determined by us and can be changed by things in real time. We can relive events, positive and negative, and wonder about how we could have changed them and question how it would have changed our lives. We can see solutions for problems that we didn't change at the time for lack of knowledge or impetus.

There is a lot less strife in the afterlife. Competition is not there. Souls are not competing for jobs, money, and power. Relationships in the afterlife are a lot easier. Souls are not looking for personal gain or for satisfaction and gratification of ego.

5

The Effectual Power of Belief

SEEING IS BELIEVING, as the old saying goes, but perhaps this can be revised as well, for I have often heard that our desire, will, and faith affect our future.

It is said that your belief brings you the reality you desire. So, in a sense, believing can result in seeing.

When you think of it, every volitional act we do begins with an intention, a belief. Those beliefs and convictions shape our lives and draw to us the conditions and reality we desire. To a degree, Shakespeare's comment in Hamlet, Act II, Scene II, which states, "There is nothing either good or bad but thinking makes it so," illustrates the powers of our beliefs. Certainly our beliefs create our own subjective reality, but also often influence the course of our objective reality.

6

Spirit Body

Souls are discrete, not diffuse, or spread out over the entire universe, are contained in a sheath, and composed of a substance which cannot be properly called matter in the sense that we know it.

Are there multiple spirit bodies or forms of different densities or vibration?

My Guide:

All are bodies, but they are integrated into one, and separate as we go along – shed as an outer sheath is pulled off, and we express our consciousness in subtler and subtler forms. These are less material, of higher or finer vibrations, and less dense as we progress.

An orb with me on the Queen Mary

My understanding is that the distinction between the physical body we know and the "spirit body" is artificial, as we essentially are all energy, but express ourselves in forms of varying density. The distinction between energy and mass is not mutually exclusive, as one can be converted to the other, and they are merely different ways in which energy can act or be expressed. Matter truly is energy, just at a lower level of vibration. Apparently the change in Spirit as it ascends in the scale of development is manifested as a change in level of vibration, or frequency.

My guide, in one of his commentaries to me, said, "You're still my kind of energy."

Do spirits have form?

Harvey's Guides:

The vestiges we retain are not physical. They are energies and morph into purer and purer forms. They are like different vibrational levels. There is a difference between the one you had before, and the newer one becomes finer and finer.

You can have a form in the afterlife and can change your form at will. At the initial transition, almost everyone has a form. Some spirits stay on lower levels because that's what they desire.

The initial transition is like a dream state. A lot of people are afraid they're going to wake up. You still hold on to who you were and what you knew on earth. Some spirits are not too sure that they have crossed over.

What are we as spirits?

Mediums and books agree that we retain individual consciousness after death. But what is consciousness? When we are alive we inhabit the physical body, but if we survive death, our consciousness is obviously not dependent upon the physical body.

So what is our consciousness? Does it have a form or substance? Since spirits do not claim to be diffusely present all over, but claim to be discreet, they obviously are a focal collection of energy, but does that energy have form or substance?

One spirit on Rebecca Rosen's television program, "The Last Goodbye", described herself as pure light. What is light? It is described by scientists as an electromagnetic energy consisting of units described as photons, but having properties of both particles and waves.

So it appears that the real me is a discrete or focal conscious collection of energy. Spirits have been described as appearing as diffuse mists, focal orbs, and in humanoid shapes similar to the physical body. Other spirits have been described as being able to assume other forms or appearances at will.

It appears that, as energy with a conscious will, as spirits we are able to assume whatever shape or appearance we wish. Spirits evidently do have an appearance and some type of finer substance, as they can appear in bodies similar to their earth bodies, in other bodies unlike the ones they had on earth, in other imaginative forms, or as mists, orbs, or other energy configurations.

Various people have seen spirits appearing as a diffuse mist, focal orbs, in bodies similar to the ones they had on earth, in humanoid bodies unlike the ones they had on earth, in other imaginative bodies, shapes, and forms, or in various forms described as light and energy anomalies, like shafts or geometric configurations of light. According to these various manifestations and descriptions, spirits can assume various forms and shapes that are manipulated at will.

Some books describe spirits as pure energy or light. Others describe spirits as capable of having either an energetic form or a humanoid form. Some refer to the Lightbody. Others refer to various forms, shapes, or bodies consisting of a finer substance or material than the physical. Shanna Spalding St. Clair's books, "Karma I and II", describe the soul form energy complex, and describe our spirits as inhabiting various finer forms and substances until we ascend completely, rejoining Source, at which time we are totally formless. So until that time we are energy inhabiting form, finer or more ethereal and subject to mental control or manipulation compared with the form we know on earth.

This offers the best explanation for me, as when they refer to spirits maintaining an energetic form, this still refers to a form, even though not necessarily humanoid. It is also stated that the spirit can assume a humanoid form or body of sorts resembling the old physical body if it chooses. Ghosts or apparitions have been seen this way and some who have had near death experiences describe their loved ones as appearing in the way they looked on earth, either in a manner in which they can be recognized, or in their prime.

This explanation of the soul form energy complex consisting of a spirit housed within various energy form sheaths or finer substances unlike the material substances we are familiar with on earth seems to account for the various ways in which spirits supposedly can manifest themselves. As Einstein described energy and matter as convertible, it would make sense that the soul, as energy, could express itself in some form of matter and form, even though unlike the matter with which we are familiar on earth.

MAKING RAINBOWS

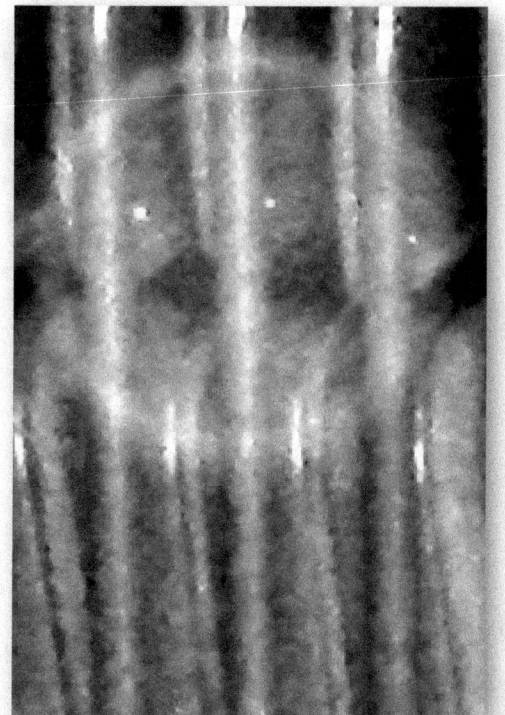

Orb of my loved one in spirit is superimposed over furniture, which creates some artifact. His face is present at the top of the orb.

An angelic orb captured at a recent seminar

MAKING RAINBOWS

I conclude that whatever form our energy takes is perceived and interpreted by our senses while in the physical body and by our spirit "senses" or sensory apparatus when we continue in spirit. Our systems for perceiving and interpreting the reality around us are designed to be appropriate to the environment in which we live. Just as the world we see, hear, and feel around us is real to us while we inhabit our physical bodies, the world we see, hear, and feel around us will be equally real to us when we continue to live on as spirits. Although the mechanisms of perception will be different, the perceptions and information we mentally receive will seem just as real and valid to us.

7

Bonds

Core differences and strength of link

There is a larger love among souls, comprised of empathy, consideration, kindness, and helpfulness.

If all of the bad things were removed from us and we were more considerate, kind, and caring; if no one actively exercised harm towards another; if all of our bad characteristics were removed and we became nicer, there would be much more love in general, one for another.

But with all of the bad removed, and if we all were nice and expressed kindness, unless our individual personalities, outlooks, interests, desires, and characteristics were eliminated, we would still have varying degrees of greater and lesser compatibility, affinity, sympathy, and closeness. We would still have greater and lesser individual preferences and loves for one another.

Among the greater consideration and love, there would still be some stronger individual bonds unless our personalities, outlooks, opinions, interests, preferences, and temperaments were erased.

However kind and loving, as long as we are different individuals, there will be a stronger compatibility and individual love between some than others. Although there is a larger, more altruistic love, my guide says that, due to our individuality and personalities, some are more intensely and intimately connected than others.

Each spirit is an individual and, as such, why wouldn't there be as there are on earth, greater and lesser compatibilities? In Charlotte Dresser's book, "Life Here and Hereafter", a communicating spirit who had been a school teacher in her earth life refers to temperament and character as the factors determining our degree of closeness and compatibility as spirits.

Spiritual compatibilities drive the depth of spiritual connections and not all spirits are equally compatible any more than they are on earth.

They just live and interact more harmoniously with greater politeness, kindness, and altruism.

Some souls share a love so deep that they make a spiritual commitment with one another to unite their wills, desires, and companionship on a mutual forward progression together, and to not be separated.

My guide states:

We love them as we do on earth, some more than others. We do have different loves for different souls based on what we're like personally and based on previous relations with them. Some are closer than others. Some choose to remain together. Others don't. It must be mutual.

We have a general love for other souls, too, in which we wish them to move forward, appreciate their kindness and what we learned from them, and wish for their welfare. That is the love of regard and kindness. But we don't spend equal amounts of time with all souls in existence or love all souls identically.

We still have individual harmonies based upon our past experiences and personalities. There are no two souls that love each other identically. There are closer sympathies and affinities, unique bonds and closer ties, all the spectrum that we have on earth, but when we lack the negatives we had on earth - for instance if two people are very different or disagree, if one is unwilling to compromise, they are not held together by the ties of marriage, as they may have been on earth. We can't exploit others for money, gain, or position as we don't need money or position. So there are no bad relationships based on greed or avarice, no relationships that we are confined in, in which the other party refuses to discuss issues or compromise, no relationships in which a difference in sexual interest or compatibility comes into play. So it is much easier to express love when we are not bound in inharmonious and unhappy circumstances.

Also there are no murders, robberies, or thefts. We can't do physical violence or rape. We can't lie to one another or cheat. When all the negative things we do to one another on earth are not possible here, can't you imagine how much easier it would be to love?

But above and beyond the forgiveness and more loving atmosphere, there still remain greater and lesser individual compatibilities and deeper or lesser bonds.

Many come and go or see one another from time to time. Those with greater differences or those who were incompatible on earth or had abrasive relationships often make peace and part, or don't see much of one another in the afterlife. Not all stay together and not all spend equal amounts of time together. It depends upon individual preference and the harmony of the souls, the law of like attraction.

There are many individual circumstances based upon souls' preferences, which remain, as our personalities and core identity remain intact after death.

8

Spiritual Change

THE BEAUTY OF change is that we can change our minds. My contact with the spirit world has affected the evolution of my thought. I was willing to experience myself as a spiritual being and, as such, contact others in spirit.

We each are on a separate journey with specific lessons we wish to experience and learn from on earth, contacting and changing from our interactions with others much as two elements in a chemical lab can come together and react with one another.

We are changed by such reactions, hopefully for the better, learning more positive behaviors and better choices from them. All of our behavior except for a knee-jerk reaction starts in thought and it is the content of our thought, our will and desire that we are changing – and subsequently our behavior.

Learning goes both ways. Those in spirit can inspire us to make better choices, and we can serve as an example to those in spirit who observe our solutions to problems and situations. They can learn alternative ways to handle problems and see the various results through us.

Spirits can reflect back upon their own physical existence and conjecture or speculate on how different choices would have produced different outcomes.

They can connect with loved ones still in the physical world and vicariously experience life through them. These are referred to as shared lives. In such cases, souls on both sides of the veil are learning and growing simultaneously. The spirit does not control the human, but experiences their emotions and life events.

The two souls are actually in spirit working together, as our mind is spirit, but sharing the experiences and learning of the one in the physical. How much closer can we be than that? Neither one is usurping the other's free will. But they can share an experience together, much as two souls in the physical body do when they are related in a harmonious and loving physical marriage.

Are we not influenced by those we love when we are in the physical body? Similarly, we are influenced by the love of those we love in spirit, and can still enjoy and learn from experiences together.

In a way I can enjoy this mutual co-created happiness, living together though on different sides of the veil by penetrating and to a degree transcending that veil - a communication that rends the veil as when we pray. We are spiritual, and the physical veil can be rent by our minds.

In that regard we are communicating and sharing mutual experiences, together in spirit, though not in the physical. It can be said that those who are mediums have one foot in the spirit world and the other in the physical world. We are living life fully, but also sharing love, communication, and experiences.

We have pierced the veil through love. We are spiritually together, sharing experiences, communication, and love, learning lessons together, loving and supporting one another in the truest sense of the word. We are all trying out options in the fishbowl, or laboratory of life together.

The true "marriage" is in the mind of two who love, want, and choose to be together, despite their circumstances, and who have elected to move forward together. Heaven and earth are not really so far apart if you bridge them through your heart and mind. There is that place in the soul where they overlap and some have found that together. Love will never die if we choose to keep it alive. We can progress together with our loved ones in that shared dimension called love.

* * *

A Close Call

Whenever you have a "close call" I think it changes you. We all know that we will die somehow, someday, but it becomes real to us when we almost do.

I'm at the stage of life in which I have been doing self assessments. Knowing about the life review and other spiritual evaluations of the lessons I learned and perhaps didn't learn, I have been conducting my own private self-assessment.

I look back at my acts and thoughts at various stages in my life and ask myself, why did I do that, was I right or wrong and why, could I have made a better choice under the circumstances, and how?

One thing I learned from those who took advantage of me or did me harm was not to let them poison me so that I became and acted like them. It is easy to feel that those "on top", so to speak, are favored, to become cynical and justify becoming like them. But if we do, we are then as bad as they are.

I have also learned to beware of repetitive, negative patterns. If, for instance, you are a person who has undergone multiple abusive relationships, it must be a lesson you need to learn, to maintain self-respect and not to allow others to erode your self-esteem. Perhaps you need to learn not to accept abuse, but to recognize that you deserve and are worthy of respect and better treatment.

Too often such predatory relationships are a poor excuse for love, and those in them are faced with the difficult choice between two bad alternatives – being abused or being alone.

Recognizing and changing negative patterns is one thing we must do as we experience soul growth. When we become less sensitive to issues and we are no longer preoccupied with them, it means we have graduated from that problem. We are healed and ready to move on to other challenges.

Even now I am ever grateful to my guide, who is so patient and gives me the strength and support I need as I occasionally relive some of the old insecurities.

My guide is also a wonderful teacher. Rather than tell me how he felt about some of the difficult situations or past trials of his life, he lets me recognize a similar situation that I have in my life, or acts with me the way someone had previously acted with him. In that way I experience exactly how he felt and draw my own conclusions. He doesn't have to explain to me in words how he felt. I live through a similar experience and know.

When you are able to come to the realization yourself, words are no longer necessary. You must live through something yourself in order to fully understand or comprehend it.

That's why we as spirits live earth lives. To think about something is one thing, but to experience it is another. That is the key to full awareness. Hopefully as I progress each lesson will be incorporated into the learning of my soul and I will have the wisdom and awareness to make the best choices possible in any given situation.

* * *

How Illness Changed Me

After having what you would describe as reasonably good health most of my life, for the first time I found myself the beneficiary of the experience of being the care receiver instead of the caregiver.

I had studied medicine and during my lifetime was the primary caregiver for a beloved dog with many ongoing medical issues some of which almost took its life, including long soft palate with many episodes of tracheal collapse, bladder stones and infection, mammary hypertrophy, hysterectomy, Cushing's disease with liver failure and encephalopathy, blindness, deafness, and cancer over a lifetime of 19 years. A former spouse suffered trials of diabetes, glaucoma, appendicitis, circumcision, retinopathy, multiple strokes, heart attacks, limb amputations and cancer, with cardiac arrhythmias and congestive heart failure.

I was a natural caregiver and accepted that role willingly and gladly, never regarding it as a burden, but rather a blessing to be able to give care to other souls.

Several years ago, during a hip surgery, I aspirated gastric contents while I was unconscious, which damaged the lining of my lungs. I had never had asthma, but after that, any time I got an upper respiratory infection I went into life threatening status asthmaticus. Recently I spent over a week in the hospital, almost dying.

For the first time I felt what it was like to watch the decline and malfunction of my own body, to see my own decompensation as one vein after another blew and an IV infiltrated in burning pain. My cough and wheezing were almost constant and I persisted for days on scattered tiny pockets of sleep. As I struggled to breathe and endured multiple antibiotics, the whole situation felt endless and surreal. For the first time in my life I felt helpless and out of control. As things spiraled downward, I finally said in my thoughts, not my will, but thine be done.

I realized what it felt like to be the patient, scared and helpless on the other side of the bed, and now knew the importance of the compassion of the caregiver. It was a definite wake-up call, as I had experienced some very callous and heartless treatment from some people in my life. This had made me guarded and cynical to an extent, and I suffered some breach of trust issues. Now I was in a position where all I could do was trust.

When I first came wholeheartedly to spirit and the pursuit of spiritual contact and development, I was in a state of profound grief, regret, and loss, and at that time made a mental contract with spirit to give them 5 years of service. As I looked blindly at my cell phone wondering where the strength for my next breath would come from, I realized that it was 5 years to the date that I had pledged 5 years of service. Not only are spiritual contracts real, but they honor our contracts.

I realize now that I had an exit point that day, one in which I had the option of choosing to walk through the gates of death or struggle on and survive. I am anything but heroic. I've always had a dreadful fear of suffocation and although I have no awareness of past lives as some people do, I suspect I may have had one in which I suffocated.

I appealed to spirit and humbly asked if I could extend the contract. Several days later something else happened. Someone brought a briefcase washed in a strong cleaning agent into my room and I went into sudden severe asthmatic decompensation, struggling to breathe. In an obviously non- accidental coincidence, exactly as this happened, there was a surgeon standing immediately outside my door, who rushed to get me racemic epinephrine and saved my life. Another elderly couple walking by who were just there to visit patients stopped and tried to help me. Spirit made sure I saw the other side of the coin, the many people we often don't notice in life who help us for no other reason than to do good for a fellow human being.

I recognized that this was a wake-up call, an insight, and a message from spirit that this is how I was to be, not at times frustrated or angry when things went wrong in my life, not occasionally overwhelmed by regrets, carrying baggage from the past, but positive about my own life, grateful that I had another opportunity to improve myself and do some good for others, no longer wasting what I now regarded as a precious gift of time to be spent well and thankful for.

Having undergone this demonstration of love during my pain, I began to think of the pain of those who helped me, wondering what they may have undergone in their lives, what trauma, what heartbreak with sufferings, and realized that, even so, they had pity and compassion on me. I wanted their wounds to be healed too, their faults to be forgiven, them to receive the love they had just shown me.

Suddenly now I could go outside myself and pray for all others that they might be blessed with love, know peace and forgiveness, find harmony and ease from pain, that they might also learn, gain understanding, freedom from harm and suffering, and grow in love, giving and receiving. I wanted those both in spirit and in the physical to know what I had just been given, a beautiful lesson in gratitude and concern for others, that they might also have the beautiful gift of unconditional love and blessings I had just received.

Suddenly I saw how I had been wasting time, spinning my wheels instead of moving forward. I thought of all the loose ends I hadn't tied up if I had left that day, of all the missed opportunities to share positive thoughts and love that I wouldn't have had. Everything I wouldn't have had the opportunity to do if I had died that day came before my eyes, and I realized there was something important I could do, rise above my own faults, be positive, and share love and kindness with others, as those in spirit and those in the physical had done that day with me.

Now I had an example to follow.

This was why I had to miss my yearly vacation and spend it in the hospital clinging onto life - to learn a far more important lesson that day- to spend the actually uncertain and brief time of my life working on overcoming negativity and sharing positive experiences, directions, and love with others, as I was in a position to receive and appreciate that day. I was now able to look beyond myself and my own concerns to feel empathy for others and to redirect my life into sharing that compassion I had just received in a more heartfelt and meaningful manner, having experienced it myself. What you have freely received it is easier to give. I had received a gift I could pass on to others.

Sometimes we wonder why we have to go through troublesome, traumatic and painful experiences in our lives. Having read Shanna Spalding St. Clair's books, "Karma I and II," the words come back to me. Be grateful for even the tragedies and painful experiences of life that provide you the opportunity to rise above obstacles and meet them with positive solutions, and that afford you the opportunities for soul growth. These are no longer just words, they are experiences burned indelibly into my heart.

9

Choices

I RECENTLY WAS IN a discussion about divorce with a friend who is a medium. There are many opinions about the ethics of divorce, and I felt conflicted about it. My friend said that, in her opinion, the injunction against divorce was man-made, and not from spirit. I had a relative who said that when the Bible states, "Whom God has put together, let no man set asunder," it doesn't mention that sometimes two people put themselves together, not God.

What happens if there is physical or mental abuse in a marriage? What if one or both parties are unable or unwilling to change or compromise? What happens when harm and degradation outweigh the good in a relationship and ongoing attempts at repair have failed? It seems that some people put themselves together who shouldn't be together. Must one or both suffer for a lifetime because of an initial mistake?

Living a double life can't be the answer, because lies and deceit are not consistent with integrity, and false pretense creates a bogus relationship, as neither party even knows the person they are with. We are what we think, so if one person doesn't know what the other person really thinks, or what they're doing, then they don't even know who they're with.

If one party honors only the part of the marriage contract that is convenient for them, the part that is witnessed in the public eye, but breaks the other vows of the contract, the contract is void. If you are living a true relationship, you don't have to hide what you are doing. Otherwise you are living a lie.

There are both legal and moral obligations. If one party upholds the legal contract of remaining together in a loveless marriage, but not the moral contract of being faithful, they dishonor and do disservice to the person they are married to, themselves, and the third party. If they choose to sacrifice their own happiness for a lifetime of misery, they should then not harm or destroy someone else's life in the process. They should not engage in a double life at the expense of someone else.

Would they want that to happen to someone they loved, perhaps their own child? The happiness and well being of all should be considered. Decisions are difficult and finding the right path is not always easy.

10

Cold Spots

When I was sitting on the couch in a relative's home, it was midsummer and very warm. The air-conditioner was not on at the moment. My relative was dozing in the recliner, and I was relaxing on the couch.

Suddenly, I felt an ice cold, focal pocket of air right in front of my face. It was so focal and so seemingly "abnormal", it alarmed me. I instantly reacted in fear, knowing instinctively that this was not something normal.

I had heard that spirits manifest with cold spots, but who was this? Was this my deceased mother, or a stranger? I felt fear and alarm and I began to pray. The cold spot instantly dissipated. I guess I will never know who it was, but that was my first encounter with a spirit affecting the environment.

I have since discussed the subject with mediumistic friends, who have also had personal encounters with a spirit causing temperature changes.

Another similar type of incident occurred while I was organizing the material for a book. I had piles of paper spread out over my kitchen table and was organizing topics into sections when I suddenly had a very strong sense of someone standing behind me. I was alone in the house at the time, and it was a very uncomfortable feeling. I didn't sense that this was a loved one or someone close to me, who would have made me feel comfortable.

I have no evidential proof, such as a picture, or an EVP recording, to substantiate what I felt, but nevertheless, I felt disturbed enough to turn around, and, of course, I saw nothing. This type of feeling coming out of nowhere has actually never occurred with me before. I do suspect that it was a spirit near me, a stranger, and I now know what some of the paranormal researchers on the televised ghost shows mean when they say the hair stands up on the back of their neck when they feel a presence or an entity. I think I most likely had an encounter with a visiting spirit in my home.

11

Commitments

THE DISCUSSION I recently had about divorce led me to ponder the subject of commitment.

When you enter into a commitment you should enter into it carefully and judiciously, asking the difficult questions, gauging the other person's behavior. You should not put other people's and dependents' lives in jeopardy because of a poor commitment or a poorly thought out commitment.

When you make a commitment, you can't say you're honoring the commitment if you only honor the part that is convenient for you. If you don't honor the whole commitment, then you're breaking the commitment. If you selectively honor only the part of the commitment that is convenient for you and acceptable in the public eye, only honoring appearances, you are defrauding the commitment. The commitment is not genuine.

There are legal commitments and there are moral commitments. If you honor a legal commitment to someone you don't love, but then break a moral commitment to not harm others, including someone you may love, then you have not done justice to the word commitment. Your commitment is a fraud or sham, as true commitments are not simply legal, but moral as well.

My guide indicates that you can't have your cake and eat it, too, when he states,

> If you are practicing infidelity, you should honor one commitment or the other instead of trying to honor both when they are contradictory, which you can't do. You shouldn't use honoring a commitment to someone you don't love as an excuse or reason to harm someone else.

I would add to that, if you are practicing deceit, you are honoring no one. Love doesn't lie. Love doesn't exploit. Love doesn't dissimulate. When you are playing both ends against the middle, you are honoring no one, not even yourself.

Honoring a legal commitment to remain together is inadequate unless you also honor the deeper spiritual commitment to respect and honor both yourself and others. Whether this is by leaving or staying in a relationship, all are entitled to respect and an attempt should be made to do as little harm as possible, but also to seek happiness for both yourself and all others involved. Hypocrisy never honors anyone. Such a solution honors only that which is in your own interest and benefit, not that which helps, protects, and is in the best interests of yourself and all others.

✷ ✷ ✷

What I learned about commitment

MAKING RAINBOWS

My guide:

The real commitment is in the heart, not on paper. If you haven't made the commitment in the heart, you won't honor the one on paper.

You can't make a commitment that is one way. The other person must make a commitment too, which includes both honoring that commitment and both providing effort to make it work. Both must work at the commitment together to make it viable.

I learned that commitment is in your heart and if you have it in your heart, it is a true one. Otherwise you have no real or lasting commitment.

Honoring something by force is a forced obligation, not a commitment.

You can't make a commitment unless the other person is in concert and then you must both honor it with your actions, words, and deeds.

A commitment is from love, not force, and love in itself is a commitment, an unwritten commitment.

What you speak with your heart comes out in your deeds, whether true or false, honorable or dishonorable.

12

Communication with the Other Side

My guide and loved one states,

It is not that difficult to do. We are living in our heart and soul what we would have lived in our physical bodies. It is possible to relive these experiences through our thoughts and intentions. Since we love each other, there is no boundary. It is that which makes our connection.

* * *

Spirit Communication in Dreams

I have had some visitations by loved ones in dreams. They were very vivid, very real, and I felt I was actually with the person that I loved. In those dreams I saw my loved ones very clearly, even what they were wearing. I could feel their emotions and touch, and hear them and converse with them word for word. These occurrences may be dreams or they may be an actual encounter in spirit, perhaps on the astral plane. In either case, they are never forgotten.

I have also had some very bad dreams. They usually consist of re-living horrible experiences I had in my life or fears associated with those experiences, and are very traumatic. They also felt very real.

One problem I have had is trying to distinguish between the two. I came to the conclusion that re-living the negative experiences in my life was a form of replaying them in my subconscious mind and trying to process them or assimilate them. The dreams I had related to fear were an attempt to overcome the fear that those negative experiences would recur. As they had such a profound effect on me, I asked my guide, are my guides giving me those dreams for some purpose, or are they a product of my subconscious mind, my own mistakes, pain, and fear? He replied that he and the other guides did not give me those dreams.

I felt that was a reasonable question to ask because I have heard of other instances in which negative spirits could influence people's thoughts, emotions, and dreams. Since my guides were not giving me those dreams, I can conclude that either I was affected by someone negative or that my own subconscious mind was reliving bad experiences I had before and fears associated with those experiences. As such, I feel these may have been a message to myself that I needed to deal with unresolved issues and determine that, based upon my own free will and decision, I would no longer accept the negative situations that led to those dreams in the first place. Essentially I needed to empower myself by saying that those dreams were reflections of the past and that by conscious decision I no longer needed to relive that past – neither in dreams fabricated and re-created by my mind, nor in my present or future life. When I became confident of my own power of choice, those dreams could no longer affect me if I had them.

I have often heard my guide speaking to me in dreams or in the relaxed mental state between full consciousness and sleep. That was always comforting, informative, and consoling. The other bad dreams were always disturbing and left me shaken. I decided that the best way to handle the recurring bad dreams, since I knew they were not being given to me by my guides for my welfare or development, was to reject them, to give them no power or validity. In that way they can no longer have a negative effect on me or influence me emotionally.

The dreams which represented visitations were always happy and peaceful and gave me comfort. I realized that I must have been sensitive even when I was young because I recall dreams like that, particularly ones in which my father was speaking to me.

I have a mediumistic friend who has also had conversations in her dreams in which guides and other spirits have spoken both to and through her, in which she has heard their voices and accents very clearly.

My friend, Harvey, was working with a man who had recently lost his wife. The man was devastated. Harvey suggested he set an intention to communicate with her in his dreams before he went to sleep and place a pen and paper on his nightstand and record the contents of his dreams when he awoke.

The man came back to Harvey later and said, "I saw and heard my wife in my dreams, and, man, did she ever give me a bunch of shit." The man had been drinking too much, and his wife had warned him in their mutual encounter.

Many dreams are visitations, and when they are encounters with loved ones, will be memorable, vivid, and loving. Negative dreams may be the product of our subconscious fears or the replay of traumatic experiences in our earlier lives. Although less likely, they could be the result of an influence of negative spirits who find that an easy way to communicate, particularly in the case of hauntings. Weakness, emotional vulnerability, and substance abuse can make a person more susceptible to outside influences.

13

Compatibility

EACH SPIRIT IS an individual and, as such, why wouldn't there be as there are on earth, greater and lesser compatibilities?

Spiritual compatibilities drive the depth of spiritual connections and not all spirits are equally compatible any more than they are on earth.

They just live and interact more harmoniously with greater politeness, kindness, and altruism.

One book, "Life Here and Hereafter," by Charlotte Dresser and Fred Rafferty, refers to it as soul ties based on differences in congeniality.

Another work, "Karma I and II", by Shanna Spalding St. Clair, refers to it as the universal law of attraction.

Matthew Smith, a medium from England and tutor at the Arthur Findlay College of Mediumship, on several radio shows, channeled two souls while in trance. They gave their names as Ling Chan and Albert. Several channeled comments included, "We go over to those we love," which implies there are some we don't. Albert also channeled that when his wife died he didn't cry tears, but when his horse died, he felt he had lost everything, and that he and the soul of his horse are still together on the other side. These comments indicate that there are still different preferences and degrees of compatibility.

* * *

My Take on Compatibilities and Incompatibilities

If two people are harming one another through their words or actions, if they can't solve their problems or accommodate their differences, if more injury than good comes of the relationship and no amount of effort or work fixes it, they may entertain the option of separating as amicably as possible, fulfilling responsibilities to others and attempting to maintain dignity and respect for both parties. No one should be bound to a life of torture or misery if circumstances are such that the relationship cannot be mended, and each should seek their own happiness and fulfillment independently. If they choose to relinquish their own happiness and remain in an unsatisfying relationship, they should not harm others as a result.

The more common interests, opinions, outlooks, characteristics, and desires, the greater the harmony between individuals— as long as their common qualities do not involve negative qualities, such as abuse, exploitation, selfishness, or lack of sharing responsibility or contribution.

Common affinities make happy pairings or relationships as long as the qualities are positive ones.

No two individuals are identical. Good relationships require some compromise to maintain happiness. Each should be concerned for the happiness and welfare of the other, and be willing to sacrifice and give. This makes happiness for both in loving and being loved.

We are each as unique in personality as our DNA or fingerprints. Two who are compatible, who harmonize, who are concerned for each other's welfare, are willing to discuss and work through their difficulties, and are able to give, have the ingredients for a good relationship.

If they have similar outlooks, personalities and interests, and feel that indefinable magic when they are together, perhaps they have the makings of that special gift, eternal love.

14

Contradictions

WHY DO SOME comments from the afterlife differ or even contradict one another?

Spirits are individuals without the physical body, and have individual opinions, as we do. They are at different levels of spiritual development, which gives them different levels of awareness. The information they can transmit is only as good as their level of understanding at that time. Spirits do not become omniscient when they die.

The attitudes and convictions of the medium may influence the message.

The degree of affinity and likeness or dissonance between the medium and spirit may affect the clarity of the message.

Perhaps there are some messages or awarenesses we are not meant to have while on earth, partly because that learning may impact or detract from the lessons we are meant to learn, or because we each have a different level of development, and we are not given information unless we are ready for it.

Also, some situations or conditions in the afterlife cannot be expressed easily in words, because they are so different, and not easily comprehended by those on the earth plane.

Harvey's Guides:

Why are there different answers from different mediums regarding the same questions?

No communication on earth or between earth and the spirit world is perfect. Many mediums develop mediumship because they have suffered a loss and wish to learn about the afterlife or become closer to those they love and have lost.

Even in the afterlife communication is not perfect and there are misunderstandings. The only thing that is perfect is Source.

15

Spirit Counsel

THESE ARE SOME of the inspirations I received when I was ill and hospitalized.

Trust in God. Thy will be done, not mine.

Forget the past. Do not become mired in it. Rather learn from it. It's over. Make your future bright with the better decisions you have reaped from the knowledge of the past.

Don't carry your mistakes with you as a burden. Realize when it's time to lay them down and be glad you won't make them again.

Be positive and prioritize better. Instead of worrying about the future, take steps and trust that if it is meant to happen, Spirit will make a way for you to accomplish your mission. Don't obsess over it because one day there may not be a tomorrow. Some things you must do in faith, and trust that you will be able to accomplish your goals. Do God's work, the work of love. God is real and merciful, but will give you an obstacle or lesson to change you for the better if you are willing and desire to change in your heart.

I do not have the same fears as before. I trust God that I will no longer have to relive the painful experiences of my past.

I am no longer bitter and disappointed in aspects of my life, but look forward to normal health as a precious gift not to be wasted, but to be used for good. I choose to live in hope and promise rather than disappointment and fear. I can empathize with others, realizing that they go through tribulations like me and are imperfect as I am, thanking them for interacting with me that I might learn from my trials, both good and bad.

I bear no malice for the wrongs done against me but forgive the perpetrators, realizing that I hope God forgives me for acts I have done in ignorance, realizing that it is better to forgive, as God does, than to seek measure for measure.

I realize that kindness and concern for one another are more important than professional accomplishment and degrees. One night in the hospital, the CNA told me of how she too was hospitalized with the same illness several weeks before and thought she was going to die, but recovered 10 days after she started to wheeze. Her story gave me hope when I was panicking and reminded me of my cousin Barbie telling me she realized when she got to the afterlife that there were kind people in her life who tried to help her, too.

I no longer look at things in such a skewed fashion but realize we are all a palate of shades of gray, and look at the best in everyone, hoping that we all come to enlightenment and strive to become the better people and souls we are all destined to be.

Given this opportunity to tie up loose ends, finish some self improvement, and do some spiritual work before I go, I humbly and gratefully accept that opportunity.

16

Diversity

I LEARNED THAT THERE is much diversity of opinion and preference, both on this side and the other side. There is always that axiom of do no harm, like the Hippocratic oath that doctors take. But aside from that, there are many opinions.

One friend puts it, "That's why they make chocolate and vanilla." Another said, "I'd be in trouble if everyone wanted my Clarky."

Some people are neat and others cluttered or slovenly. Some have very different interests and some very different personalities. Some have very different desires or interests, expectations or compatibilities in a relationship. That's why some become our best friend or greatest companion through thick and thin, and others we seldom see, don't connect or feel empathy with, and some we have friction with. All are not for us.

This becomes apparent in the widely differing personalities and beliefs of each person. There are some we relate to instantly and with whom we form a soul connection. Others we don't feel harmony with.

Even in mediumship there are many opinions. Some connect with guides and others find it irrelevant. Some believe the sitter will benefit if they can ask their loved one a question and get an answer through the medium. Others find that distracting or inappropriate. One medium put it well in my perspective when he said, regardless of how good you are, you can't be everyone's medium. Your idiosyncrasies and traits make you more appropriate for some than others.

This is true in life as well as in mediumship. We are drawn to those of a like nature and disposition. One fit isn't for all. We are pulled or more sympathetic with those with whom we resonate most strongly. It's like magnetism. We are happiest with those of a like mindset, personality, and character, both spiritually and physically, with the spiritual predominating on the other side as we don't have physical bodies. All things mental and spiritual stratify us as a centrifuge.

17

Forgiveness

What is my guilty pleasure? Ghost shows. I've been made fun of by other mediums for watching them. Some people feel they're all fake or dramatized and others feel they have no redeeming value. I can't say every show or person is authentic, but I can say I know there are real mediums. Evp's are real because I have one I recorded on a closed loop of white noise that can be listened to before and after, and the Evp is clear and not present on the original closed loop. I also know orbs are real. I captured them with my own camera on the Queen Mary. The Ovilus can also be real as I got intelligent responses on it from my loved one. That doesn't make every person or show real, but I know what I have gathered for myself is real.

When I was young many mediums were ostracized and publicly condemned. They were regarded as frauds or crooks. I remember saying that I knew my grandmother, who was a medium, was real, and if there was one real medium in the world, then mediumship was possible and there must be others.

I'm not writing this to convince you. I'm writing this to say that if proof of survival is important to you, then you should find the answers for yourself as I did.

No matter how much my friends tease me I always learn something from the shows. One I particularly liked recently was Kim Russo's "The Haunting of Karina Smirnov". My favorite aspect of it was the lesson of forgiveness. As I hope to be forgiven for the errors I have made, I recognize that others who have hurt me have also made mistakes as I did, and if I hope for others to forgive me I must also be able to forgive them. In addition, I can't move past my mistakes if I can't forgive myself, and if others can forgive me, then I also should be able to forgive myself. Mistakes are for learning so that you don't have to make them again. I'm not perfect, but I'm trying to improve, and that's moving in the right direction.

One difficult thing is forgiving someone who continues to hurt you because you are in a situation that is extremely difficult to get out of. I guess that for many reasons we all have to put up with some difficult situations in our lives, and must try our best to forgive those who misuse and harm us, attempting to keep a positive attitude as much as possible in spite of mistreatment, and attempt to rise above anger. This is not easy, but if the consequences of getting away from the situation are dire, perhaps in practicality this is the best you can do. When others continue to do me wrong I try to remember the good and positive things I have and remind myself of the lessons I am learning and how not to get into that situation ever again. That is merely attempting to make the best of it, and something that at times we all do.

A particularly difficult issue was addressed recently on medium Rebecca Rosen's show, "The Last Goodbye". It was the case of a woman who had been horribly murdered by her deranged son, and a daughter who was left behind with conflicted and tortured emotions. From the other side, the mother commented that she was able to forgive the son, whom she described as a wounded soul. I give kudos to those on earth who can forgive such heinous crimes. Perhaps on the other side we can come to an understanding that is more profound that escapes us while we are confined in our mortal framework.

18

Fulfilling Dreams

CAN WE LIVE out a very important dream on the other side that was unfulfilled in our lifetime, as long as we don't harm other souls?

My guide states:

We can relive our thoughts and memories or live out our wishes and dreams. We have the ability to fulfill our deepest desires. We have the ability to create sensations without a physical body. We can create and receive sensations and perceptions, feelings and imagery, sounds and understanding, in our spirit form. A hallucination feels real to the one hallucinating. These ideas and perceptions do not have to be physically engendered or based in order to be experienced realistically by a spirit. We can have anything we want as long as we don't harm others. You'll see.

MAKING RAINBOWS

Can we fulfill desires that were never fulfilled on the earth in the afterlife?

Harvey's guides:

There's no reason why they cannot be fulfilled in the afterlife. In the lower levels, you can replay parts of your life that were very negative or positive and possibly relive them and use your free will to live and experience what you missed.

These experiences will feel real to you.

19

Dying

What is the difficult part of dying?

Harvey's guides:

The difficult portion is like a flash. People may try to hold onto life because it's all they know. You're numb at first, and then you find out you will still have a connection with those you left behind. You become more comfortable, especially when you find out you can communicate.

20

Energy and Einstein's Equation

Since we are energy manifested in form and my loved one on the other side has referred to me as energy; since the progress we make on the other side is referred to as ascending vibrational levels that correlate with our words and actions; since it has been said that we choose our station or level of development in the afterlife by our deeds and thoughts in our current life, I have noticed an interesting correlation with Einstein's theorem and equation.

It has been described in Shanna Spalding St. Clair's channeled book, "Karma II," that as souls we experience successive incarnations after death into finer and finer energy sheaths referred to as energy form soul complexes. The channeler says that we maintain form, meaning discrete form, not necessarily humanoid, until we reunite with Source or God.

Einstein's equation $E=mc^2$ indicates that a given amount of energy is equivalent to a given amount of matter times the speed of light squared. So if you elevate matter to the square of the speed of light it transforms into energy.

We are said to increase in our vibrational level as we ascend through the levels of the afterlife, assuming a finer and more rarefied form as we go. It would correlate with Einstein's equation that when our vibrational frequency or level speeded up to a maximum point we would then become pure energy. That would be the point at which we reunite with Source. Souls in the afterlife have also been referred to as having bodies of light. Light is a form of energy, consistent with this hypothesis.

Similarly, as energy can be converted into matter, souls can assume denser forms by expending their energy to do so, lowering their vibration to express themselves in a denser form of matter.

21

Afterlife Environment

ARE THERE BUILDINGS, nature, appearances, and activities in the afterlife that are similar to those we know on earth?

My guide:

We can create those things if we wish to. Those are all within the realm of possibility.

On earth, we have set forms that we can manipulate. We have earth, nature, trees, stones, mud, sky, gasses, elements, all of which can be manipulated into houses, building materials, chemicals, medicines, and objects. These are more set in form on earth. They are more fixed, or structured.

On the other side, there are realities and forms beyond what we experience on earth. We are able to change the forms of the spiritual environment more easily. They are more malleable or fluid. There is a more organized reality on earth. More fanciful environments are present in the afterlife, with surroundings created from thoughts. Thoughts, not hands, manipulate the afterlife environment, which is more plastic.

An impressible matter is present that is responsive to thought. The afterlife substance or matter is more sensitive, that is, sensitive to control by mind. It can be shaped like clothing. Particles like atoms are the building blocks of the substance or "material" on the other side. These are receptive to or influenced by thought/mind. These are not matter as we know it on earth, but a spiritual form of material.

22

Experience, Life's Best Teacher

MY GUIDE IS a wonderful teacher. He is one of the best teachers I've ever had. When it comes to understanding issues and problems, he doesn't just give me the answers or give me advice. It's one thing to receive advice or explanations and comments, but it's another thing to live through the experience yourself and realize your own conclusions.

That's the way my guide has taught me. He has led me into a situation or made me think of a circumstance in my life that involves the same issue or problem he had that I'm now confronting, and lets me realize the answer by living through the same emotions, myself, and drawing my own conclusions.

That way I will have achieved insight into a situation or problem by relating it to a personal experience in my own life. That makes the situation real to me and I can feel or empathize with how others may be feeling when addressing the same problem.

For instance, he has made me feel like he felt by placing me in a similar circumstance or situation, and then it will dawn on me and I will realize, oh, now I know how he felt. What a brilliant way of showing me, rather than just telling me. Now I know how he felt, I don't just have to imagine how he felt. I don't just hear words, I feel feelings.

Until you feel something yourself, experience something yourself, you never know precisely how another person feels going through that same experience.

I think that's why we have to come to earth to learn lessons. On the other side we may be told something, but until we experience pain, betrayal, loss, lies, and all the other insults of life, we cannot fully comprehend them. We know them in our soul when we have lived through them. Until that time, they are just speculations, thoughts, imaginations. But when we live them, they become real to us.

23

Feelings and the Bigger Picture

I AM TRYING TO reconcile two warring aspects of myself. The feeling part of myself regards the loss of my loved one as a tragedy. On an emotional level I can't be happy at losing the love and companionship on a physical level.

The intellectual part of myself reasons that there is s greater purpose and I can be thankful for the lessons and soul growth for each of us subsequent to and because of that loss. I am grateful for the resultant learning that benefitted my loved one and myself.

That is true but does not eradicate the excruciating feelings of emptiness, loss, unfulfillment, and hopelessness. On that level, from the feelings in my heart, I wish I could be with him physically and had never lost him.

The other less selfish part of me is grateful for whatever benefit may have come to him as a result of the loss.

Those two factions of me exist and are each valid. I wish I could spend my life with him now in the physical but would sacrifice that for his welfare and benefit because I love him.

Unselfish love, the love we strive toward, does not seek its own gratification, but the welfare of the beloved.

24

Moving Forward

Kim Russo, on "The Haunting of Margaret Cho", commented on the conclusion of her reading that it is necessary to let go of the pain of the past before you can move forward.

It is like the Bible said, "The dog has returned to his own vomit or the pig has returned to wallow in the mire." Change isn't instantaneous. You have to cross point A before you can get to point B.

If I were to speak to those who injured me in the past I would say, "I forgive you for the harm you did to me. I hope you forgive me for any harm I caused you. I made a mistake when I got involved with you. I now recognize my self-worth. I will never get involved in a relationship again where there is no love. If you love someone, you don't deliberately or carelessly hurt them. In the future I will only get involved in a relationship where love is mutual, in which I love my partner and am loved by him." I am changed by my experiences and will never relive anything like them again.

Perhaps that is the purpose of having them – to recognize them for what they are so that we don't have to repeat them.

25

Maintaining Individual Freedom

IF YOU ALLOW yourself to be manipulated by another person who is domineering, you will be reduced to a drone to fulfill their selfish purposes. You will be subservient to their own selfish needs and fulfillment. Your happiness will be sacrificed to theirs and you will merely be their pawn.

Although you need to fulfill certain obligations to other people, this falls within reason. It does not mean that you must entirely sublimate your own needs, desires, and happiness, to the fulfillment of someone else. It means that there is a compromise and a balance, and if that balance is not achieved, you will be consumed by others who have no concern for your welfare.

Living a lie or subterfuge while attempting to find happiness covertly is not the answer. We have an obligation not just to others, but also to ourselves, and that means not only fulfilling obligations to the best of our ability, but also living an honest life. No one is required to be a martyr.

I learned in my lifetime that there are some things that cannot be entirely overcome. I also learned that you can't avoid all unhappy or negative relationships because people lie and don't put their cards on the table. You have to assess their true intention by their actions, and if their actions are suspicious, you must address or discuss those issues with them. If they shout and refuse to discuss the issues you know that you have a person who is domineering, unwilling to give, and demands everything their way. They are unwilling to compromise and you are there simply to fulfill and meet their needs. Your needs will neither be met nor considered. That is the time to determine whether or not you want to continue that relationship.

I also learned that involving other dependents is unfair to them unless you have a stable partnership with someone who is spiritually compatible with you. Otherwise they partake of the unhappy consequences.

It is apparent that nothing is black or white. We are all shades of gray with good and bad, and we must seek those with whom we are most compatible, both physically and spiritually, to be our companions. As no two individuals are identical, compromise will always be necessary. We must seek those with whom we have affinity, compatibility, and then work at the relationship together to create mutual happiness.

Life isn't always fair, circumstances are not always fair. We must work and strive for that which is most valuable and most precious. In the end, nothing else will make up for what is most important. I learned that good pay, good jobs, a nice home, a good education, the fulfillment of artistic pursuits or other creative or intellectual interests and accomplishments, do not make up for the lack of a happy relationship. I discovered that nothing in the world, the entire world itself and all it has to offer, cannot make up for the lack of love. Nothing in existence can replace or make up for the absence of a happy love relationship with someone I love, who also loves me. This is the one priceless commodity that can never be replaced by anything else. This is my formula for happiness.

Having this, even in the eternal form, which, at the end of the day, is the lasting form, is fulfillment and contentment for me. When the illusion I am living is over, the true and lasting joy and peace will be mine. Knowing and having that is true happiness for me. May you be blessed to find and achieve your true happiness.

26

Spirit Gender

RE SPIRITS INHERENTLY male or female?

The answer I have been given is, "No ". They have no set gender, but based upon their experience, some may have a preference for a male or female role.

I am told,

> A predisposition, preference, or predilection for the role of "male" or "female" can be inherently in our spirit on the other side.

What constitutes male and female on the earth?

One thing that defined men and women was the roles they played. The traditional role of a man was defender and breadwinner. Those roles and distinctions are no longer clear cut, because there are now many women who are the sole heads of household and breadwinners, and there are many men who are caregivers and Mr. Moms. So the old traditional roles are no longer applicable in defining men and women.

Another thing that defined men and women was their anatomical, biological body differences. This is not entirely clear-cut either, because men and women can now have sex change operations that alter the anatomy they were born with. In addition, spirits no longer need the sexual organs, and the anatomy that defined men and women on earth is no longer relevant. In addition, it has been suggested that spirits incarnate as both men and women at various times, so we all must have male and female potential or qualities within us.

Another way of distinguishing men and women has been to classify men as more aggressive, dominant, or stronger, and women as more gentle, passive, or weaker. This cannot be seen to represent a definite qualifying characteristic, as when mediums are giving readings, sometimes they mistake male spirits for female and vice versa, saying, "This spirit has a strong male feel, or a soft feminine quality." Oftentimes in training, I have seen a psychic who is seated and blindfolded attempt to describe someone standing behind their back. The one thing they most often get wrong is gender.

This leads me to the question I had. Are spirits created as male and female, or do they have an inherent predisposition or predilection for being a male or female?

The answer I got is this.

> We have both male and female attributes in us, since we incarnate as both men and women. When not in a physical body, this is an artificial distinction. However, some spirits prefer one role or another.

We express some of our attributes in any given lifetime, and express those attributes, or a certain set of our attributes, in form.

We have certain personalities that dictate our preferences, so we can express those preferences at will. We can therefore be said to have a male or female predilection that is a result of our choices, which are a result of our personality. But we are a combination of "male" and "female" traits or characteristics. They in turn contribute to and direct our behavior. They express themselves in our behavior.

So we are a combination of male and female characteristics, but may express one or another in our form, and we may have an inherent preference or predilection for one or the other role.

We can be said to have been created with tendencies that direct us or predispose us one way or the other. Our inherent disposition and character gives us leanings and preferences for a male, female, or neuter role. The farther away from the flesh we become, the less these distinctions would matter. They become artificial labels, and are no longer relevant as we progress on the other side, but distinctions can be maintained as long as it is important to the individual.

We can say that we are created male or female to the extent that our inherent nature makes us choose or act in conformance with one role or the other, or an ambiguous neuter role. We often have a desire for one gender or the other based upon our own personal nature. So some people are said to be more male or female based upon which quality or temperament is dominant, more prominent, or in ascendance, and is thus expressed.

In essence, we control or affect our shape and can change it at will on the spiritual plane. We can assume a bodily form that is real, and can be seen or touched by others on the spiritual plane. It is a morphing of our substance into a particular shape, a manipulation of our energy sheath. We create, or make a substance to project ourselves into with our energy and guiding thoughts. Form is plastic on the other side, not fixed. And energy is transmutable into matter, as Einstein's equation indicated. We can use our energy to assume matter or express ourselves in matter in whatever way we prefer.

27

God and Related Philosophical Topics

INSPIRATIONS FROM THE spirit world:

There is a God who is greater or stronger, an intelligent, loving consciousness that is all of our finest qualities perfected.

We all can be seen, that is, if we choose to manifest a form, and if we can, that means God can, too.

God is a reality to us because we live in an environment of love and spiritual law. We are aware that there is a greater source of creation and life.

God is the origin of all that is, the intelligent, loving creative force from which we emanate. There is circumstantial evidence of an origin, a creation, a purpose, and an intelligent design.

We partake or consist of the same spirit or life force as God. God is the author of all, and there is a purpose in our existence.

God is the creative force, the spirit, the consciousness from which we originate, and runs the show. The spirit in us is of God.

We are of the same spirit, life force, or material as God, yet a separate consciousness, identity, or will.

The spirit in us is of God. God does have divine laws and we have free will within that framework. The same spirit of God resides in us, but we are individual conscious souls. God is the supreme Guide.

We are similar in our constitution but separate in our expression.

We are the energy of God with a separate will and consciousness. But there is progression. That implies intelligent design and purpose. So God is more than a blind force. It is an intelligent design with moral values and the emotion of love. As God is described as love, God must have awareness, and as there is described progression, that implies a design, a purpose, an intelligent foundation and plan, an understanding or intention.

If God is love, God has emotion. If God is the creative origin, God has power. If there is guided progression, God has intelligence. If God shares the spirit within us, God is a spirit. If God created us and we didn't create God, God is above us. If we are meant to learn and make better choices, God has or exhibits moral values. If there is order, there is control or management. If God has love, God must be conscious. If God created us, God must be intelligent.

God is separate from and greater than each of us, yet we embody or contain the same spirit and life force, and maintain an individual consciousness, intelligence, and will.

If God created us and we are male and female, God must have created us as male and female. Therefore we have a purpose as such in a body. If God created humans he must understand humans. If we are learning, there must be something that is better and worse, or then there would be no need to learn. There must be a higher or greater understanding and behavior. God is in control and we have freedom designated to us within limits. If there is order, there is control.

God is greater than us. He created us, not the other way around. God is the all-encompassing intelligent, conscious, loving creative spirit of all existence, of all the manifestations of energy. We come from God, are separate wills and intelligences, but derive our life force from that same spirit of God and share God's spirit within us.

* * *

Right and wrong

The fact that we have a life review and progression implies right and wrong.

* * *

Preservation of individual consciousness

Since we learn from events, we do retain our individual consciousness and perspectives. Otherwise there would be no need for or purpose in learning.

* * *

Those on the other side are still learning

Since you recognize in your life review that you could have done things differently, you continue to learn on the other side and can change your mind. You work out emotional issues with others in your life and learn forgiveness.

* * *

Right and wrong

There is a right and wrong since the whole process is about gaining awareness and making better choices. The fact that life is a school and we are learning lessons and growing or progressing implies that there is a right and wrong thinking or behavior, a better or worse.

* * *

Spiritual hierarchy

The fact that spirits cannot or are not permitted to harm one another and that there is structure, learning, and progression in the afterlife implies that God is in control. It is not haphazard or anarchical. There is direction and purpose.

* * *

Guidance

The fact that there is a Life Review and a direction or guidance, a growth, and a greater learning, wisdom or understanding, as well as levels in the afterlife that our energetic vibration or frequency ascribes, assigns or confines us to, implies that God is intelligent and directing. There is a greater plan.

* * *

Levels in the afterlife

Our energy frequency that our thought patterns emit and our behavior confines, commits, or assigns us to a certain vibrational level in the afterlife, a localized plane. Our behavior selects our position. Our rate of vibration correlates with our level of development. There is magnetic attraction. We are separated into levels of existence or consciousness by our vibration/signature.

* * *

Evil

The "evil" lose power. You can't intimidate, coerce, or harm a soul.

* * *

Thoughts are things

When they say two souls are co-creating, it means they are cooperatively choosing and creating their future circumstances and conditions.

* * *

Self-respect

One of my lessons in this life was to learn not to mistake kindness for self abnegation or allow others to demean me, to not permit or allow others to shape my opinion of myself or to negate my self-respect.

* * *

Teachers

The fact that there are guides and teachers means there are wiser choices and greater understandings.

* * *

Roles

We accept roles together to learn. I won't use the word play, because that sounds like we are adopting a phony persona, someone who is not us. By accepting roles I mean we agree to interact with another to experience circumstances that will change us and help us to grow and learn.

* * *

Coincidence

Nothing really happens by coincidence. There are causes for everything. The event may not be a conscious choice, but nevertheless was precipitated by previous actions.

* * *

Forgiveness

I harmed you. After I can accept your forgiveness of me, then I can forgive myself. I forgive you for any wrong you have done, as I, myself, wish to be forgiven.

* * *

Negativity and positivity

If we change our beliefs, we change our behavior and lives. That is how we advance. Negativity is confining. Positivity is expanding.

* * *

Karma

The nature or vibration of our energy, it's direction and control-how we use it-produces changes in our lives. That is karma, the results of our actions, which are the result of our thoughts. We can change the course and direction of our existence. We must be willing to do so.

* * *

Positive thought

Positive thoughts engender positive experiences. Think you can and then you create the behavior that helps you to attain the results, the experiences, the outcome.

MAKING RAINBOWS

* * *

Thoughts are things

That is why they say thoughts are things-because they produce actions and conditions. Thoughts have energy. Magnetic attraction applies. Like attracts like.

* * *

Energy

Your energy, your choices create events. Lack of love and respect for others creates wrong or harm toward others.

* * *

Does God Speak to Us

My guide:

Some people who have had near death experiences and some children who claim to be reincarnated say that God has spoken to them. Can God speak to us?

God can transmit feelings, thoughts, and words. God is capable of understanding us and communicating with us.

What are we made up of? Energy in varying stages or levels of vibration, the physical being most dense, but our thoughts are energy also. They are things. The physical things we see around us aren't the only things that exist. Things that are not in our auditory or visible spectrum are nevertheless things. When Einstein said energy and matter are interchangeable, this indicates that energy must also be a thing.

Our feelings, perceptions, and visual images are things – our energy and our individual consciousness is defined by our unique thoughts, feelings, and interpretations. These are our energy signature and identify us as accurately as our physical appearance and vocal quality do on earth.

If God has a purpose, God will speak with us in thoughts, ideas, feelings, or words. God can correspond with us. We can be impressed with thoughts, visions, and feelings by spirit.

If you can receive my thoughts and feelings, why not those of God, a more powerful spirit? So that means God can communicate with us if he wishes.

How can we know if it's God who has spoken to us or another spirit? Discernment – spiritual "reception" that our physical ears will not know. We have to respond and interpret with our own spirit.

You heard a brief message five years ago and felt but also wondered if it was from God. That message was not meant for me to hear. It was meant for you to hear, and when you expressed it, I heard it.

We are sharing teaching and learning experiences. I learn from your reactions to what I have taught you. It is a complex action and reaction process. We learn from each other's thoughts, expressions, and feelings.

Can God speak to us audibly?

Harvey's guides:

When we pray to God, we speak to him directly. Yes. Sometimes it can be audible. God speaks to all of us. We can't prove that he doesn't. It can also be in deeds, things that happened that can't be explained. Too many things go unexplained as far as practicality to be denied.

We also respond. We do it by doing good deeds, trying to live a good life, and meet him halfway. God is the purest of spirits.

28

Mediums and Grief

You'd think mediums who are in touch with the other side and know there is a life after death would be less shaken by grief than the average person. Not necessarily so.

I recently lost a dog unpredictably at an earlier than average age. I have lost several dogs before at an advanced age, and, although painful, there seems to be something particularly disturbing about losing one earlier than expected, particularly when the dog has not lived a full life.

In fact, in retrospect, I had gotten a warning of sorts from my medium friend, Karuna. She called me out of the blue one day and said, "Penny, I don't want to alarm you, but I'm getting a very strong feeling about one of your dogs and sickness. I'm also getting a sensation of asthma."

Well, I have a dog that has had some breathing issues after I boarded her in a kennel, when she unexpectedly got exposed to cotton defoliant sprayed on the surrounding cotton fields, and she had to be intubated with emergent respiratory distress.

As days went by and no problem occurred, I filed the message from my friend in the back of my mind and forgot it. But then one day my other dog started having episodes of transient blindness when she went out into the sunlight. My regular veterinarian was stumped and before I could get her in for an appointment I had made at the university teaching hospital, she started bleeding internally from an immune related thrombocytopenia and passed away shortly after receiving a splenectomy. This was a huge shock for me, and I had prayed long and fervently for her recovery.

I realized three things from the incident. One is that, in hindsight, I did receive a cryptic warning from my friend, and the asthma referred to me, as I had had several asthma attacks from emotional distress while driving her to the university.

The other is that not all prayers are answered with a miracle or a yes. And the third is that when we lose someone we love, mediums have human emotions of grief, just like anyone else. Because I know there is a life after death, it gave me comfort that my dog was okay and that I would see her again on the other side, but I mourned her early departure and missed her physical presence acutely. It felt like there was a big hole in my heart and an emptiness in the house.

A wonderful veterinarian who has had her own challenges with health issues sent me a lovely condolence I wanted you to hear. She said, "You don't get over it, you get through it." And I thought, how simple, yet how profound. You never really get over the loss of a loved one while you are in the flesh. You will always miss them and your world will never be the same. But you get through it in the sense that you continue living and forge ahead despite your grief. The grief is still there, and you still have to deal with it.

29

Guides

GUIDES ARE SUPPOSED to guide us. What does that mean? Does this mean, influence us to make sure our lives are on track regarding certain important milestones we set up for ourselves before we were born, such as meeting a future husband or wife, going to a particular school, or selecting a particular career?

Imagine if we missed one of our important choices, how that could change and affect everything else that subsequently happened to us, and possibly get us off track for our life's purpose.

Also, if the guides give us too much guidance or information, then we would have an inside track, so to speak, and never feel the consequences or weight of our personal decisions. If we were just "given" all the answers to the test, we would never learn the lesson.

So I think guides have an immense responsibility in walking a fine line between influencing us too little or too much. They must make sure we encounter the situations we planned to learn from, meet our designated milestones, but retain our free will to make the choices we learn from in the process. Harvey's guides said they impart wisdom. But our choices must be ours.

MAKING RAINBOWS

My guide states that the objectives of a guide are to keep you on track with your purpose, help you focus your energy in the right direction, and give you some counseling and wisdom if you seek it.

* * *

Guide Requirements

My guide:

In order to be a guide, we have to have prior experiences that have given us the understanding of how to overcome obstacles.

The person who can connect most deeply and help someone overcome a problem is one who has experienced and overcome that problem themselves.

30

Habits

HABITS ARE HARD to break because they are thought patterns that become ingrained in our consciousness like rote or repetitive learning. They create a magnetic stored impression, as we may recall an old memory or stored detail from bygone years.

It is stored in our minds, not just our brain, and we can access the stored thoughts to a greater or lesser degree depending upon the emotional importance we assign to them. When a thought or feeling or fact is repeated, its impression is strengthened. We are able to recall it more easily. It is more deeply etched on our consciousness.

I am told that since we have recall of our experiences and life events after we die, that mind and consciousness are a part of the soul and not solely dependent on the physical brain.

Likewise, patterns of behavior are more difficult to eradicate because they are "programmed in" and it takes a conscious decision and volitional concerted effort to bypass them and create a new behavior. That's why it is easy to fall into old behavior patterns and why it is difficult to establish a new action or coping mechanism.

When we have a thought pattern or behavior that no longer benefits us or serves our highest purpose, it takes a conscious decision and prolonged effort to change it or replace it with something better.

31

Healing

WHEN IT COMES to the subject of healing, I am somewhat conflicted. Although I believe that healing does exist, I have never experienced it myself. A friend of mine who is a medium and who I will refer to as D., recently asked me if I knew a good healer I could refer a friend of hers to. I said "No, I didn't," but began to think about the subject.

Some time ago I had been to a physical mediumship demonstration in another state and had felt someone touch my forehead as I sat in complete darkness in a locked room. I was told it was a famous healer, now deceased, but the next day, when I shook hands with the physical medium, his hands were small, cold, and perspiring, just like the hands that had touched my forehead in the darkness the night before. So I was very skeptical.

Another time I had a different medium give me a healing session, but my ailment remains unhealed today. Although I have never, myself, experienced a physical healing, I have seen others healed.

Many years ago a friend of my deceased relative was healed of terminal cancer in a church and also underwent a complete change in her personality, as well as a complete transformation of faith that changed her life completely, instantly, and dramatically.

I knew her. She lived another 20 years cancer free until at last she went home to God.

A second instance occurred in the church I attended for many years. A lady with lung cancer was prayed for fervently and she went into remission, living another three years of joyous pain-free life.

But I was hard pressed to recommend a healer, so I asked my friend, Harvey, what his guides said about the subject.

They said the person essentially heals themselves, and that the healer doesn't heal a person per se, but facilitates the individual to heal themselves by accepting and believing that they can be healed. His guides also added that group energy or prayer can contribute to someone's healing and that, certainly, God has performed miracles and healings throughout history.

But they also said that a person needs to have a positive outlook in order to have a positive healing outcome. Sometimes it is a person's path not to be healed, but to suffer illness or die. As my friend, Harvey, put it, God always answers prayers, but sometimes the answer is no. Otherwise, no one would ever be sick or die.

My medium friend, D., said she had attended a healing session some time ago and felt the healer was not genuine, was a showman who profited from gullible patrons. In response to my question about all of these healers, religious or otherwise, who claim to perform miraculous healings, Harvey got the message, "Elmer Gantry." This is the title of a movie I had not seen but which depicted a fraudulent healer who was exposed as a conman. This does not mean that all healers are charlatans. However,

I am sure, as in any discipline, there are those who exploit healing as well.

Also, before I consult anyone for advice or help, I always try to assess whether their life is in order and how successfully they have addressed the problem that I have in their own life. For instance, would you get advice on how to rob a bank from someone who is in the pen for life? Would you take cooking lessons from someone whose food is so bad, even the dog won't eat it? Would you get dating advice from someone who is a permanent resident of Heartbreak Hotel? I prefer to see if someone has solved the problem in their own life before I ask them how I can solve my problem.

The same is true with healers. Are they in good health? Do they have their emotional issues under control? Do they have it together? If not, I'll stick with the man upstairs and ask for help from a higher source.

32

Humor on the Other Side

I WAS REMINDED OF how a sense of humor doesn't die when someone passes to the other side. I was at a Tony Stockwell trance class when we were paired up to give readings to each other. Our assignment was to give a message by incorporating a form of trance and allow the spirit to come into us, so to speak, and merge with our auric field. In that way, we could give a more detailed reading as we temporarily "became" the spirit.

I was paired with a young lady and as I sat with her I began to experience some trouble connecting with a spirit, and she said, "You know, I don't have any dead people. I only have dead animals." At that point, I thought, OMG, I have never brought through an animal before, and now I have to become one.

So as I tried desperately to relax, who comes to me? Not an ordinary dog or cat, which I could relate to, but two parakeets. I thought, how am I going to become a parakeet?

That's when I gave up and trusted spirit, and sure enough, I started to have parakeet dying issues, and then felt like a free parakeet going through parakeet emotions. I realize that, on some level, we can identify with any spirit.

As I started to feel like a bird (I didn't start tweeting) my partner said "Yes, yes, yes." So that was Spirit's way of taking me out of my comfort zone and having a laugh and a little fun with me. But guess what? For those few minutes I was a parakeet, and I have to say I'm glad I lived through that experience and earned my badge of courage.

33

Identity

IF WE DIDN'T maintain our identity, we wouldn't learn from our experiences. If we didn't retain any awareness of who we were, how would we learn lessons and improve ourselves if there is no continuity of individuality or personality? What would be the purpose of progression? If we were instantly changed and perfected by death, why would we need to continue learning and progressing, or come to earth in the first place?

If there were no right or wrong, better or worse, there would be no need for progression. If there is no right and wrong, why progress?

If we didn't recognize the significant people that we knew in our lifetime when we go across, there would be no sense in having a life review or forgiving one another. If there were no continuity of relationships, there would be no way we could learn from one another or discuss our prior lives. If we didn't know one another on the other side, it wouldn't make sense when mediums say that families are together or that a mother is with the son who died, or that a grandparent is with a child who passed away early. Sometimes it is said that a husband-and-wife are together on the other side, and sometimes it is stated that they are separate. There would be no need for love if there is no continuing love relationship between people who continue to maintain their individuality and to recognize one another.

If we didn't know or recognize those from our past life or lives or between lives on the other side, there would be no continuity of relationships and no need for love. Why would love be important if we don't continue to know people – those we've loved?

If there is no continuity of relationships and love or no special love between certain souls, why do our loved ones specifically come back to us in spirit circles? Why do mediums always say, "Your mother and father, deceased child are together or with grandparents, or your brother is with your grandfather", if no one knows or recognizes their earth acquaintances on the other side?

If we don't recognize each other, what is the need for a life review? How can we discuss our prior lives with our earthly relations and forgive one another if we don't even know each other?

It doesn't make sense to say that all souls love one another equally on the other side. Would my friend love her abusive father as much as her beloved children? Would another dear friend love her despicable ex-husband as much as her adored son? Not all souls even know each other. I have heard mediums say that a certain soul met up with another in the afterlife. Why is it that our loved ones come through most often in seances rather than our distant acquaintances or complete strangers? If it is said we are the same people, just without a physical body, doesn't it make sense that some people get along better with each other than others, that some are more compatible than others? If some have much deeper bonds of love in this life, wouldn't that certainly be the case in the afterlife as well?

Must all love be impersonal, just kind deeds toward all? Is there no persistent bond between individual souls that lasts, no special closeness or love between certain souls who have developed that closeness through their past experiences, or are drawn together by their unity of nature, personality, and thought – who share an affinity?

If we are closer to some people than others on earth and love some more deeply, wouldn't it make sense that we would also have some we are closer to in spirit? If we retain individuality, individual consciousness, identity and personality, why not? We are not equally bonded or compatible on earth, and I am sure that persists or translates into the afterlife.

I'm sure we love more, are kinder, knowing the effects of our actions on others, but if we remain individuals with separate identity and consciousness, I am sure some are more compatible or have more affinity than others.

If we don't need to eat in the afterlife, don't need to sleep in the afterlife, don't have a physical body to take care of, houses to maintain, children to raise; as there is no house or family to provide for materially, no house to clean or children to raise, no physical goods to purchase, no material possessions to buy, most of the time occupied by these pursuits on earth would be free in the afterlife. What, then, do we carry with us into the afterlife if not the physical body and all things accompanying it? The only thing that we could take with us is the knowledge we have accumulated, the lessons we have learned, the relationships we have established, and the love we feel.

* * *

Soul, Spirit, and Identity

The soul is described in Shanna Spalding St .Clair's book as a soul form energy complex.

The soul is the individual unique core identity or personality. The spirit is the life force in each one of us that has its origin in God. The personality, emotions, mind, beliefs, and intellect are the components in our soul that define us, shaped and polished by our experiences.

We each have some form until, and if we choose to reunite with Source and become formless. We are made up of energy inhabiting form.

Our consciousness is our inheritance from Spirit and is our self-awareness. Our mind is the thinking, perceiving aspect of our soul. Our energy, directed by our mind, may dwell in different, discrete kinds of form and transmute itself from one type of form to another as we progress along our spiritual pathway through our subsequent incarnations.

The will is the ability of the mind to determine its personal actions and choices. Love is one of the qualities of the pure or discarnate soul before it takes on the energy sheath of the human body. Reasoning is the ability of the mind to interpret its surrounding circumstances and reality.

There exists energy throughout creation which is plastic and can be conformed to matter, which in turn can be manipulated by mind.

* * *

Individual Identity and Reunion with Source

Do we maintain individual identity when we ascend and reunite with Source?

While all the atoms and molecules in a tree are part of the tree, the whole, yet each atom and molecule remains distinct. When we reunite with Source we are an expanded consciousness, yet retain the individual consciousness, memories, and selfhood of the identity we had. We are not obliterated or less than we were. We are expanded or greater than we were. Our thoughts and feelings are not annihilated.

How can we be happy or why would we be happy if "we ", our identity or consciousness, no longer exists? It exists as part of a greater whole in which our identity is merged, with which we are united.

34

Other Dimension Incarnations

DO WE INCARNATE along the course of our evolution into other worlds or dimensions?

My guide:

We do have the ability to incarnate in other realities with the consent of our advisers. These other realities include physical and nonphysical dimensions of a different sort from that experienced on the earthly plane.

35

Maintaining Integrity

Y̲OU HAVE TO learn to stand your ground so you aren't consumed by others' wishes and desires for fulfillment, to the exclusion or subservience of your own. If you relinquish your own free will, fulfillment, and goals to satisfy others, you are allowing them to control your future rather than shaping you own soul's destiny. Each of us has a purpose, a plan, an accomplishment, and only we can determine whether or not we pursue or achieve it.

You must also preserve integrity in your work, or its efficacy will ultimately be compromised. When you have pride in the work you do and the work is rewarding; when you love what you do and your work is not just for sustenance, your achievements will reflect the care that went into your effort. This is true in both career and personal relationships. Going through the motions or putting up with something because you feel compelled to do so will never produce the stellar results you can have from a labor of love.

36

Learning From Life

KNOWLEDGE DOESN'T ORIGINATE in us. Awareness does. Source or God is all knowledge, but we are coming into awareness of that knowledge gained through experience - knowledge not just believed, but known.

Life is the revision and fine-tuning of our thoughts through our ongoing experiences.

Truth falls into many categories. There is a truth that consists of knowing the facts, or knowing the actual feelings and thoughts of another. There is a truth that encompasses physical matter and natural law, which can be measured and reproduced. There is an emotional truth of subjective principles and convictions which we each uniquely interpret and espouse. These truths are privately held convictions and values.

Love is the deep regard and appreciation for another person that we share through our actions. It is the going outside of oneself and one's own interests to seek the welfare of another, to cherish that soul for who they are, sharing our emotional connection and experiences together with them in mutual regard and endeavor - a giving of oneself and a receiving of the other in mutual caring, concern, shared endeavor and pursuit. It is the intense emotional bond that we share together and manifest in our deeds, words, and actions. It's dedication and commitment to the relationship between yourself and another. It's sacrifice of the self for love of another.

37

The Lesson

My medium friend, D., received a lesson in a dream from my guide. A portion of it went as follows.

> I entered a classroom and looked at the professor with glasses and asked
> "-----??"
> Teacher: Please call me "teacher" when you are in the classroom.
> Teacher: Have you been doing your homework?
> D: I'm not sure.
> Teacher: Well, you'd better get sure. I don't want to waste time here.
> D: What can I learn?
> Teacher: Everything. Nothing.

Tapping on the blackboard for attention.

> Teacher: We will begin.

MAKING RAINBOWS

I was aware that I was not the only student in the lecture hall, but I was in the first row and it would have been rude to turn around.
Teacher: D., come to the board and show us what you have learned.

I remember walking up to the board, and I don't know what I did or said,
but there were new diagrams all over the board.

Teacher: And remember, nothing will happen until you begin.
    Don't be afraid.
    Don't be lazy.
    Don't be consumed with your ego.
    Don't waste your heart with sadness.

Teacher: Open your heart. Fill your soul.
    Learn to fly. (He threw a paper airplane at me!)
    Help those whom I love.(****this was strange to me because you expect to hear- help those you love....
    but he said help those whom I love!! He handed me a roll of pennies)

It was a large lecture hall/ auditorium, with a large platform deal reaching around in front of the chairs, the kind of lecture room which has a blackboard all along the front wall.

There were jars of specimens on the table and calculations all over the blackboard.

My response to the friend who conveyed The Lesson was, I think we have our work cut out for us. I have a feeling our lessons will continue until graduation day!

Always remember, when you get discouraged, that even though those on the other side have the BIGGER PICTURE, they are learning, too. They even learn lessons from us, - what we do right and what we do wrong.

But it made me think about everything.

I made a balance sheet in my head. On one side I thought, I have the man of my dreams and his love. On the other side I thought, I have some nefarious people and a small amount of pain for a short time. As I thought about it, the love got bigger and bigger and the pain got smaller.

Then I remembered that the Bible said in the flesh you will have tribulation. In Me you will have peace.

And then Shanna Spalding St. Claire popped into my head. She channeled, "You must be grateful even for the painful experiences you have and view them as an opportunity to grow and develop as a soul."

Finally, I concluded that what really matters is the love, and what can I do that is positive to spread joy the rest of my life. The bad things aren't going to disappear and go away. They are part of life in the physical world as long as man is imperfect.

So I decided, they can't steal my joy in the Spirit. They can't even see it. As long as they act in the flesh, they won't know it or have it.

So with my renewed attitude I've resolved that I'm going to spread joy as much as I can and live in the strength of my relationship with spirit and then I will have made something of this lifetime to be proud of.

Life is short. Oftentimes we don't realize it until it is almost over. Even in a long lifetime, what are 90 years compared to eternity? How often we waste precious time in ignorance and trivial pursuits. I am as guilty as the next person. That is why I love the poem by the 19th century poetess, Emily Dickinson,

MAKING RAINBOWS

I had no time to hate, because
The grave would hinder me,
And life was not so ample I
Could finish enmity.
Nor had I time to love, but since
Some industry must be,
The little toil of love I thought
Was large enough for me.

38

Life Lessons

DO WE HAVE specific circumstances planned for each incarnation based upon our soul's needed lessons?

My guide:

We have an intent for each incarnation, a lesson or lessons, a purpose that will enlighten us and provide us with soul growth and direction.

What were the life's lessons of my primary guide and my current guide?

> Harvey's guides:
> Compassion and commitment

Since we have free will, can we deviate from our planned life's lessons?

> Harvey's guides:
> We absolutely can deviate from our life's plan and lessons.

A spirit channeled in Charlotte Dresser's book, "Life Here and Hereafter", writes, "You see, "Here life is one of experiment and growth, failure and success, pain and pleasure, privation and privilege. But all of these qualities are weaving themselves into a strand of experience and wisdom. Don't you see? Character forming even through our mistakes and blundering. Never dwell on the darkened past except to let it lead you into brighter paths."

39

The Purpose of Life

What is the purpose of life? I'm sure that we have all pondered this at times.

I believe that God does not want us to do good or elect to do good by default, but rather by a conscious, aware choice. The only way for us to learn that the spiritual principles lead to happiness, and not the inclinations of the flesh, is to allow us to experience harm at the hands of others. By knowing how it feels to receive harm, we will choose not to do harm.

My understanding of the purpose of life on earth is that we are meant to control the physical inclinations with the spiritual, to learn to desire the things of the spirit, and to recognize that the spiritual principles of love – treat others as you would have yourself treated – live in peace, joy, in the spirit of Source – lead to happiness, not the selfishness of the flesh.

On the other side we do not have physical bodies, so we do not have physical urges, nor the opportunity or ability to hurt or inflict harm upon others. We can't hurt one another. The desire to rob, steal, cheat, lie, murder, kill, and dominate are not applicable. These are ineffectual, and cannot be implemented in spirit.

Certainly God does not want us to be good just because we have no choice and because spirits can't harm one another. He wants us to learn to choose to do good by ourselves, suffering the effects of harm in the physical so that we willingly elect or choose to do good, knowing that the principles of love, kindness, truth, honesty, and joy, lead to happiness rather than selfishness, injustice, exploitation, green, hatred, inconsideration, lying, cheating, stealing, abusing, violence, murder, and disregard of feelings.

One psychic medium from the television series, "Sensing Murder", a psychic detective series based in New Zealand, commented that from her relationship with her former husband she learned the feeling of hatred, and, asking her guides what the purpose of that was, was told, if you didn't know what hate feels like, how would you know what love feels like?

When I was being given a lesson several years ago by my Spirit Guides I was presented with a situation devised by my guides that had a profound effect on my life. As it is very personal, I won't discuss the details, but it is one of the most significant learning experiences I have ever had, and one that will persist in my consciousness for as long as I exist – that is, for eternity. At the end of the lesson, I heard the words, "Now I know what it feels like." Only because of living through this lesson will that knowledge be present within my soul – because I experienced it firsthand.

40

Spirit Life

Spirit communication and effort

Any communication that we have, anything that we do in the afterlife will not be through physical or material means, but through mental activity, through vibrations and mind. Actions and accomplishments will occur through harnessing energy, through mental direction and force. It will require learning to use new methods and new tools. It will require exercising new senses and applying new concepts.

The mind is the creator. The physical body is the mediator in the material world. In the spiritual world, a physical mediator is not required. The mind will directly receive transmissions and information and will directly produce results in the surrounding environment without the necessity of the physical senses, organs, and limbs. All will be mediated by the creative consciousness and energetic mind.

* * *

Purpose of earth learning

What is the purpose of earth learning, since we can't harm one another in the afterlife – we can't lie – we know each other's thoughts; we can't kill or inflict physical pain – we don't have a physical body; we can't steal – there are no physical possessions or money; we can't cheat– there's nothing to gain or steal; we can't dominate another soul into service – there is no way to intimidate or threaten, and all have free will; we can't rape – there's no body for sex?

We are in an environment that prohibits wrong or harm. All that we can have is negative thoughts – that is, wish to harm or desire to inhibit or cause mental pain and anguish or unhappiness, and these are ineffectual. We cannot force someone to do our will, belittle them, or harm them mentally. We cannot deride them.

The purpose of undergoing these things on the earth plane must be that spiritual law has to be written in our hearts, and the only way we can choose or appreciate kind and benevolent treatment, is to experience the opposite ourselves, and thereby learn to treat others as we would like to be treated. Who would want someone to treat others morally or make good choices only when someone else is looking? We ourselves would want someone we could trust to "do the right thing" just because it is the right thing, not because they were forced or shamed into doing it.

* * *

Afterlife destinations

We are drawn by our quality of thought to a level of vibration compatible with our thoughts, desires, and intentions, one based on whether we have negative or positive thoughts toward others – helpful or harmful thoughts, selfish or unselfish thoughts. We are learning to progress and control our thoughts, for these create our deeds.

* * *

Spirit occupations

What occupations do spirits have since there is no need for food production, factories, manufacturing, financial institutions, medical care, production, or law-enforcement?

What do spirits do since they don't have a need to provide food, shelter, and clothing? They have no need to work for a living to sustain the physical body, no need to nurture a family, clean the house, cook food or raise children, which occupy so much of our time. They have no need to eat or sleep, to maintain a physical body. The eight hours of work and eight hours of rest are unnecessary, so what do spirits do or occupy themselves?

They partake in the equivalent of many familiar earthly activities and more. They enjoy learning, relationships, leisure, and explore opportunities to help those they love on earth. There is a spiritual equivalent for many earthly pursuits and enjoyments.

Occupations or, better put, endeavors and pursuits or avocations, are determined by ability and interest, and spirits can engage in helping others to learn, helping others to develop areas of interest, intellectual pursuits, or character development, artistic endeavors, or anything to promote mental growth or well-being, learning and productive creative endeavors, understanding subjects and relationships, promoting creativity and artistic expression, among other options. Helping those on the other side and earth are important, sharing knowledge and fostering abilities.

* * *

Spirit senses

Since we won't have the physical sensory apparatus for the input of our environment, how do spirits receive visual, auditory, emotional, or touch sensory input from the environment? How do they get knowledge of their environment and communication – visual, auditory, and tactile?

They transmit thoughts, images, feelings, and "touch" sensations directly through thought vibrations, which do not need a network of sensory stations or nerves to be conveyed to the other person (soul's) mind. All of the things in the physical, the input from the environment, are translated at relay stations of sensory receptor cells in the ear, the eye, the nervous system – which receive and interpret energy vibrations. All are waves or vibrations interpreted through our sensory receptor cells and translated into mutual apprehended visual images, auditory words, sensations, and feelings by the mind. In spirit we receive those vibrations directly and they are interpreted without the need for a physical relay system. They are received directly by our own vibratory receptor mechanism of our mind.

* * *

Spirit Enjoyments

The things we do for enjoyment on earth – the visual stimulation of a movie or artwork, the auditory stimulation of music, can be directly created in the environment by mind – the harnessing of vibrations and channeling of energy, and received or interpreted by mind. The sense of touch such as used in sports can be re-created or "invented", as can the gustatory senses of taste and smell if desired or wished to be experienced. The experience of dancing, golf, or baseball can be created and enacted, as the sensation of touch.

I am told that these perceptions will feel real to us, whether the circumstances are actually created or are produced by a manipulation of thoughts and the mind, such as a hallucination. In either case, they will be perceived as "real" by us.

* * *

Spirit expressions of affection

How do spirits express affection and intimacy? They can re-create the sensation of touch or sexual union, or they can merge energies in an intimate sharing of thought and emotion, expressing a complete oneness more intimate than the physical bonding or sharing of sex. They can experience a complete blending and knowing of one another, a union and oneness of passion, feeling, and thought.
 Together they can create an experience of intense electrified bliss or rapture, a shared experience of ecstasy more profound, loving, and intimate than the earthly sex act. They can together engender in one another shared awareness, emotions, and sensations beyond the excitement and bliss of orgasm.

* * *

Spirit intimacy

Are there are degrees of closeness among spirits? Yes, but they are not determined by physical appearance, but by emotional makeup, intellectual interests, common qualities of mind, opinion, feeling, personality, desires, outlook, and inner mental or emotional qualities. They are driven by an emotional or mental compatibility, a commonality of thought and desire, a harmony of personality and emotion. There are deeper bonds of love between some spirits than others based on prior experiences and mental and emotional makeup or harmony.

* * *

Spirit relationships

What are relationships like on the other side? The relationships are as spirit or soul peers, not as parents, children, husbands and wives, because those roles are not needed. The relationships are as those of loving brothers and sisters, without an age or gender label, without an expected duty or occupation, without a specific dependency. Souls are sentient beings acting and reacting with one another as peers, "friends", loved ones, without the labels of husband, wife, mother, father, and child, in varying degrees of love, beneficence, mutual concern, and intimacy, based upon compatible ideas, thoughts, desires, interests, opinions, emotions, and individual personality and goals.

However, if souls desire to relate to one another in certain roles, such as a family hierarchy, or a paired relationship, such as spouses, they can also experience or continue that type of relationship if they wish.

* * *

What is the place of ego on the other side

The ego is the aspect of ourselves that promotes anything selfish done for the purpose of self gratification, not for the welfare or care of others. Its primary focus is to aggrandize the self, such as in the pursuit of fame or success, that feeds the self importance and self preoccupation.

On the other side ego is diminished. The selfish human concerns dissipate and are replaced by genuine concern for others.

A certain amount of ego is necessary for us to develop our personalities or produce accomplishments on earth. But the more selfish aspects of ego experienced on earth are reduced on the other side.

41

Loss and Karma

KARMA

Our thoughts, emotions, and deeds are energy. Karma is balancing out the energy, the effects of our thoughts and actions. We integrate the total body of our experiences, both negative and positive, to learn from them and improve and grow as souls. Karma creates conditions for us that are the sequelae of our thoughts, words, and deeds.

* * *

Reflections

I began to reflect on the adversity and tragic loss I have had in my life, and began to ask, why did this happen for me? The answers I got are as follows.

I now realize that there is no such thing as bad luck or coincidence. When I underwent the loss, I felt complete meaninglessness, utter hopelessness and despair, dark nothingness and emptiness, the knowledge that a life without love is not worth living, a world without love is not worth living in.

I have come to realize in the grand scheme of our lives that we must experience multiple outcomes, both the negative and the positive, in order to learn to choose the best option available to us. I had to learn the lesson that there is love, and life is valuable beyond what we can see in the physical.

I had to find out that things that seem unfixable are fixable. The loss changed my focus to a spiritual endeavor, a different purpose, emphasis and direction. I had to feel that I had lost love in order to recognize that a life without love is not worth living. I had to subsequently find out that love never dies, and to develop the strength to persist on the foundation of spiritual love, to develop faith and strength, to realize that we never die and there is always hope, to realize we have the power to make life what it is. We always have the ability to improve something that seems hopeless or helpless.

We will be able to relive things we did wrong and make them right. I found out that we always have the ability to change, and that we are not the victims of fate, but can shape our own destiny even in the most adverse of circumstances or conditions. I learned to believe and make it reality. I learned that wishes do come true if we believe they can. I learned that we can turn or change the worst into the best, that light can come out of darkness, and that nothing is hopeless, even if it seems so, that nothing is impossible for those who believe, and that true love wins, triumphs in the end. I had to learn that when love, trust, and self-worth are taken away by uncaring people and adversity, they can be gained again. Nothing good is ever lost eternally. We have to look to spirit to find it and believe the solution or enlightenment, the path lies within our own soul, that restoration of all things is possible, and that love never dies.

* * *

Love Beyond Words

Jeffrey marks book, "The Afterlife Interviews, Volume II", states that some tragedies and losses are preplanned in the spirit world before incarnation to act as catalysts to move people along. It required such a loss to force the survivors to incorporate new areas of experience into their lives. The person who is lost is playing a martyr, almost. These people could actually be spirit guides coming to play that role.

I now realize that the loss I endured was not the act of a cruel God or cruel twist of fate, a cold and impersonal or meaningless accident. It was a profound act of love, a love greater than any words could convey, that gave me the opportunity to learn things that I could otherwise never have learned. Someone loved me enough to give up their own happiness and joy of living to help me learn the lessons I needed and grow spiritually. How truly unspeakable it is to be loved in such a way.

I learned that a little drop of love is better than all the riches in the world.

42

A Love Story

THERE ARE DIFFERENT forms of love. There is first the love of all souls for one another, which is the love that we express when we train or teach each other in our life relationships, the love of kindly concern, compassion, helpfulness, brotherly love, the helping hand, peace and harmonious coexistence.

There is also the individual or personal love we feel for another soul with whom we have great affinity. This is the love that we have when we get along with someone, the chemistry we have with someone with whom we have more in common. That produces a closer connection, greater attraction, a deeper love and stronger commitment, a unity or communion. This is the personal or individual love of empathy and compatibility, togetherness. Those are the souls we wish to remain with, those with whom we have deeper bonds of love and harmony.

What makes a good love story? Drama. Action. A hero and heroine who get separated, overcome tragedy, and live happily ever after. Two lovers who pledge eternal love and sustain their love through the most difficult of circumstances. Each learns and grows as a result of difficult life's lessons and both come together at last, united in true and eternal love.

Well, I wrote one. The only caveat is that I penned it somewhere in the afterlife before I came to earth. It had all the ingredients of a great drama, all the twists and turns of a Shakespearean plot, and I was the heroine.

In the plotline, the true lovers meet, fall in love, but get separated by fortuitous circumstances and death, and are then reunited to find true love and lasting happiness. That's what happened to me.

I could never have foreknown the heights of love and rapture, the depths of loss and despair, before I lived them. They are now a part of my eternal soul.

I suffered and I overcame. I lost my dreams and then I lived my dreams. I found out the full meaning of hopelessness and despair, and then I discovered eternal hope and fulfillment, finding out that true love can triumph over the direst circumstances.

But every fairytale has a happy ending, right? Well, this one does, too. After losing the love of my life through a mistake and a series of unfortunate coincidences, I found him again in the most unpredictable way, after he was dead.

I once read a saying in the Bible when I was young. Love is strong as death. I believed it then and I know it now. Those are no longer just words inscribed on a page, but truth engraved in my heart.

In my obsessive-compulsive way, I would edit one word. I would say love is *stronger* than death. Death can never take away the love two people have for one another unless they allow it to.

We are now reunited and I am living out the love I've always wanted with the man I've always loved. We have celebrated our union together with an eternal vow.

Drama. Check. Tragedy. Check. Confounding circumstances. Check. Twist of fate. Check. Loss and despair. Check. Unforeseen restoration. Check. Miraculous reunion. Check. True love. Absolutely!

Now for the ending. Well, there is none, really. She rode away on her Prince's white horse into the sunset to live and love forever.

I wouldn't have written it any other way.

* * *

Do all spirits love one another?

Several visiting spirits in a recent Spirit Circle brought home a similar point. They were both here for a woman who was a houseguest of my medium friend, L. I brought through her guest's biological father and Harvey brought through her stepfather. She was astounded, and said they hated each other in life. How was it possible they would come through for her together? We were given the understanding that each now respected the love that the other had for her. They had both put aside their differences and come through to support her. It wasn't about them, but her.

Her biological father gave me a beautiful insight. He said, "We each honor the best part of each other." How aptly said.

43

Spirit Manifestations- Hallucination or Reality

I HAVE SEEN MANY ghost shows on television, some celebrity testimonials, some descriptions of encounters by ordinary people, and some documented footage from paranormal teams.

Many people have reported seeing solid looking apparitions. Some have reported interacting with them, believing they were living people. Various people have reported seeing them, talking with them, riding in a car with them, and even touching them. Many mediums who have experienced the gift as children report having been frightened or confused, not knowing how to distinguish dead from living people.

Although I personally know that the spirit world exists, I wondered whether these spirits were manifesting in a solid body, a physical body identical to the one they had on earth, or whether they were presenting themselves through a hallucination in the mind of the perceiver. So I asked my loved one and guide.

He states,

> We can have bodies that are similar to our earthly bodies, but not identical, and they can be felt and touched.

We can manifest in a body like that, but it requires lots of energy and it is very difficult for us once we have crossed over and have higher vibrations, to lower them enough to be perceived on the physical plane.

It's not always possible, but can be assisted with energetic help if there is an important need. When spirits remain near the earth and have not crossed over, it is possible to assume a form like their earthly form at a lower vibration, which can be seen and sometimes even touched by those in the physical. It is not identical to the physical body in constitution and function, but for all practical purposes looks and feels like the physical body to those interacting with it.

Even on the other side, we can inhabit a spiritual form or assume a body in which we can do the familiar earthly things, such as talking, touching, kissing, and hugging. All these are possible and require our desire, choice, and effort. There are more possibilities and choices on the other side than in the fixed materialistic environment of the earth.

A friend of mine, L., who is a medium, states that information she received from spirit indicates that on each spiritual plane, the spirits inhabiting that plane can see and touch one another, in essence, feel and appear "solid" to one another. But those at a higher level of vibration may not be seen, as most of us on earth do not routinely see "dead people". She states that those on a given level can see and feel others on that level.

44

Love and True Marriage

IF THERE IS no one who loves, who truly cares, who means what they say, what is life worth? If there is no trust, there is no relationship. There is only false pretense.

A relationship founded in falsehoods is a sham. Any relationship not built on the truth is an illusion, a deception, because you don't even have a valid, real relationship, only something phony, something not genuine, only something you mistakenly presume exists. If there is deceit you don't even know who you have. How can you honestly love someone if you don't even know who they are? You mistakenly love the person you think they are or imagine them to be, not the real person they are, whom you don't even know.

If there is disrespect, unkindness, falsehood, there is no love, only a deception or pretense.

A true marriage is not a marriage on paper. It is a spiritual marriage if truth and love live in the heart. If you don't love the person you are married to, the marriage bond is already broken. All you have is a binding legal agreement that forces you to stay with them physically and fulfill monetary or financial obligations.

You have already broken the marriage vow to love, honor, obey and be faithful to them, if you do not love them. You do not love them if you lie, deceive, cheat or are unfaithful. If those vows are broken, the marriage vow is broken. The true spiritual bond is already dissolved and violated. Only the legal bond or agreement forcing you to stay together or adhere to financial obligations remains. In such cases the true spiritual marriage bond is already broken and disrupted, negated. Only the legal tie, a paper contract of law, remains.

Love is the eternal law, the true marriage in the heart, for if you truly love someone you will not cheat, deceive, lie, harm, use, or otherwise disrespect that person. If you present falsehood or deceive, you do not love them and have violated the marriage bond, the true law. Love doesn't mistreat, use, deceive, break trust, lie, cheat, demean or otherwise mislead. Love is kind, considerate, caring, honest, faithful, and true. When love is gone, there is no marriage, only an empty shell that forces people to be together in unhappiness, deceit and false pretense.

In Charlotte Dresser's book, "Spirit World and Spirit Life", Dee and Mary, communicating from the spirit world, state that the marriage contracts formed on earth are dissolved and only the true tie of spiritual love continues on the other side. Only if the bond is spiritual does it persist.

45

The Real Me

WHO AM I? Who is the real me, given that I've had other reincarnations as male, female, different races, genders, physical bodies, and circumstances? What is the real me behind all of these costumes?

I am wearing a body right now. I am experiencing a particular environment, culture, set of relationships, expressing myself in a particular language, and experiencing life as a particular gender. These are all artificialities, or superficialities.

I am not that body, gender, or culture. I am experiencing those circumstances but I am the thoughts, feelings, the personality that interprets and undergoes those experiences. I am the consciousness behind the cloak. I am the identity of my thoughts, opinions, desires, likes, dislikes, abilities, convictions, and temperament that make me "me".

That is the eternal yet ever-changing essence of me. I may change opinions, beliefs, attitudes, and behavior with additional ongoing learning, but there is a core identity, a unique reasoning consciousness, a distinct personality with my own ideas and feelings, that comprises, identifies, and defines me.

That is the eternal individual "me". These thoughts, these feelings are my own. They belong to and are engendered by my consciousness.

I am in that sense a creator, the author of my own values, creations, acts, feelings, and ideas. I am the director and author. And I am always honing, refining those skills, always improving me.

The culture we absorb and act in from one lifetime is not that important. It's the lessons we learned that we take with us for eternity, and are continually refining.

My respected and beloved teacher, Robert Brown, gave me a reading years ago from my loved one in spirit, and said, "You will never meet anyone exactly like him again." That is to say, we are each a unique, irreplaceable individual, no two of us exactly alike. Another medium, A. J. Barrera, also bringing my loved one through, said, "He's still a character on the other side." A. J. captured his fun-loving, outgoing, engaging personality perfectly, along with other detailed aspects of his persona and life. It was comforting to me to know that I will meet up with the man I knew and loved, and that his personality is still intact.

* * *

Since I have had many reincarnations with different genders, races, roles, appearances, and occupations, what is the real me that lasts eternally?

MAKING RAINBOWS

Harvey's guides:

The real me is the soul, which is constant. Spirituality – one's relationship with Source stays constant. As you ascend, the particular characteristics of a given lifetime become less and less important.

Your individual characteristics don't go away. They just become less important. There is no amnesia or obliteration of yourself. There is a general shift in priorities, but specifics remain.

We all are individuals. We are like a piece of pie, cut from the same general pie, similar, but not exactly alike. Your relationship with Source and others you come in contact with makes you who you are. The soul evolves.

The lower levels of the afterlife are very similar to souls as when they left the earth. They retain vestiges of any given earth personality, but the details become less important as they advance.

46

Finding Meaning

Have you ever had one of those bad days where everything seems to go wrong? Like one on which several people have been downright nasty and unfair and another has been completely unscrupulous? Well I had one recently and my view of humanity was particularly dim. I was pondering, why on earth did God create mankind when so many are abusive, devious, liars, unfair, and exploitive? I just couldn't see the good for the bad and was very depressed.

That night in spirit circle I got quite a surprise and an important lesson. My cousin, Barbie, who had severe emotional trauma when she was young, and quite a difficult life, came through with a message.

None of the mediums knew what I had been thinking that morning, but Barbie knew, and addressed it directly. That shows me that people on the other side know what we're thinking and are there to help us. This is not the first time she answered a question I had in my mind but never expressed openly.

She gave me the message that although she had a difficult life and made some choices she later regretted, she said since she arrived on the other side she realized there were many good, kind, giving people she met in her lifetime, who were there to help her.

No one could have delivered that message better than she did. I realized, if someone who had more than her share of trauma, problems, and heartache could find the best in people, and recognize love, kindness, and caring in what seems often to be a cruel, selfish, cold world, I could certainly find the same.

I had just been exposed to some heartless people who used and deceived others, but those people had skewed my viewpoint and clouded my perception to the point where I wasn't sure anyone honest and caring existed.

Of course that's not true, but it took that observation from someone who led a harder life than myself to reawaken me to that awareness. Whenever I see someone nefarious in the future and am tempted to believe that kindness and love don't exist, I will remind myself of what Barbie said.

47

The Medium – Spirit Connection

WHAT DETERMINES THE strength of connection between a medium and a spirit?

The depth of a connection can depend on how experienced the medium is, what faculties the medium possesses, how accomplished a communicator the spirit is, how well the medium can effectively set aside personal interpretations and biases, and how synchronized a connection there is between a particular medium and a particular spirit.

It can also be enhanced by a love bond between the two. It takes a lot of energy and motivation to come through.

What makes a stronger connection between the medium and a spirit?

Harvey's guides:

1) Respect. When you are a medium you are in a precarious place. Most people don't believe in it. We have to

MAKING RAINBOWS

respect the information we're given and deliver it as it is given to us.
2) We need to get out of the way. Spirits are trusting us to pass the information on the way it is given. Trust works both ways.

48

Accuracy in Mediumship

How difficult is it for mediums to get details correctly? Fairly difficult. For example, Kim Russo, on "The Haunting of Audrina Patridge", is linking with a spirit at a Chicago bar, and recognizes a relationship between two spirits, a man and a woman. She states that she feels that the woman was probably his wife. The man had murdered the woman in 1907. A photograph of the local newspaper article of the time was provided and show the two last names blacked out, but one was significantly longer than the other. It was apparent that the two last names were different. It is only in more recent times that women have begun retaining their own last names after marriage, so was the woman his girlfriend rather than his wife? I think details are very difficult to convey accurately.

When my medium friend, Karuna, was at a Robert Brown seminar in Virginia Beach, she was called upon to "play act" a demonstration of ethics in mediumship, and she was to play the medium. Much to her surprise, as she opened her mouth to speak, a spirit came to her and spoke through her, saying, "I am so thankful for the chance to speak with my loved ones again and assure them

I'm all right, I don't mind if the medium doesn't get the message perfectly. I am just so happy and thankful to be able to communicate at all."

My friend, Harvey, was receiving a message from his guide and I asked the same question. His guide responded, "It's very important to me to get the message through accurately." So there you go. Differences of opinions still persist on the other side.

I recently had a wonderful opportunity to unexpectedly speak with Eric Medhus, the spirit who has channeled information to the world through two books, the first of which I have read, which is called "Channeling Eric." I have heard that he also communicates to us through a blog site run by his mother. I had happened to call my medium friend, L., and she mentioned to me that Eric would be featured on an upcoming radio show. I was delighted, as I had found the book comforting and informative, and I especially like the fact that, although many channeling spirits have exotic names and they communicate lofty philosophical messages, Eric has the ethos of a regular guy, and I feel many young people as well as older people, can relate to him so easily.

I casually said to my friend, "I wish I could ask Eric a question. If I could, I'd ask him – it's so difficult for mediums to get all the details when communicating, is it hard for the spirits too?" Well, to my surprise, my friend said "You know, he's listening", and, to my delight, he answered the question through my friend. He said, "It can be a real pain in the ass sometimes." I was thrilled that he answered my question. I feel that he and others work so hard to give comfort and reassurance to many in grief, and I like his cheeky attitude and how he is down-to-earth, so to speak, and has fun with the communication. Thanks, Erik.

My friend also stated that after she had prepared to do the radio show, she was driving home from work and stopped to run an errand. While she was in the parking lot, she felt a strong emotional state come over her and blurted out some words she would never ordinarily have used. She then said she got it. She realized that it was Eric overlaying his own emotions on her that he had experienced on the earth plane and he was putting his words into her mind. She both heard and felt what he had been feeling as well as sensations that he had near the time of his death. Eric is known for pranking people, and I laughed hilariously at the words that had come out of my friend's mouth which were completely out of character for her, and her complete astonishment until she realized what was going on. Even now, when I recall L.'s reaction and words, which were a total surprise to her, I dissolve in fits of laughter at Eric's prank on my friend.

49

Mediumship

DIFFICULTIES IN MEDIUMSHIP

Do you know of anyone who is perfect? Do you know anyone who has never made a mistake on their job? Well, mediums aren't perfect either. All of them occasionally get something wrong, depending upon their level of experience and ability.

I recall one medium who is particularly accomplished and renowned throughout the world giving me a reading in which he stopped in midsentence, paused, and reworded what he was saying entirely. Later, when I became more advanced as a medium, I asked my loved one on the other side whether the original wording or the corrected wording was his. When there are questions or possible inconsistencies, I typically ask my loved one to confirm which option is correct by moving my hand, repeating the answer in different words, or by using the divining rods. In this manner I try to eliminate as much subjectivity as possible.

I did ask my loved one which wording was correct and he indicated that the corrected one was what he had in mind, not the original wording. So all mediums, even the most experienced, can occasionally miss things or present them in a manner that gives the wrong connotation. This is something that cannot be entirely avoided as we are human and communicating with the spiritual dimension. As Paul said in the Bible, "We see through a glass darkly."

In the same reading, that same medium also gave me a phrase from my loved one, saying, "These are his exact words. He's telling me not to change a single word." If something is crucial, the spirit can expend great effort to get their precise words through to the sitter.

Another situation that mediums can encounter that can be confusing is when several spirits come in at once to communicate. Often times they have similarities and many of the statements can be taken for either one. What the medium has to do in this instance is separate them and go back-and-forth between them, giving statements, comments, and evidence pertaining to them, one at a time. I have been in the situation, and have grown to feel the difference in personalities and comments. In those instances I was able to discern who I was speaking with. It can be difficult, however. I have seen mediums who are highly adept and accomplished do this with ease.

An exercise in this vein is one in which a medium has to get up in front of an audience and establish multiple contacts, putting each one on hold and going back-and-forth between them to get evidence from each one, one at a time. I saw this done with great facility by a young medium in a class I recently took. It was absolutely astounding to me to see how easily she moved from one spirit to the other and back again. She never missed a beat.

But, on the other side of the coin, what if you aren't getting anything? Some sitters are just plain difficult to read. It could be for multiple reasons. Some people don't have anyone close to them who has passed and others may not have a deep connection with those they know who are in spirit. Sometimes the sitter may have a closed off energy or protective shield. There may not be resonance or an open connection between the medium and sitter. I have encountered several different people who were nearly impossible to read. Interestingly enough, I discovered that other mediums more experienced than myself also had problems establishing connections with their deceased loved ones. One famous medium described the time he just handed a woman's money back, saying, "I'm sorry, I'm not able to get anything for you." Since mediumship appears to be as much an art as a science and is difficult at best, it is not surprising that some connections just can't be made. I've found that as a medium, possibly depending on your physical or emotional state, how tired you are or how distracted, there are good and bad days, days when you're on and receive information easily, and those where you feel as though you're "pulling teeth", to use a colloquialism.

There are also some controversies and differences of opinion when the communicating spirit makes comments not just pertaining to themselves and their relationship with the sitter, but also makes comments about the sitter's life. Some mediums feel that this is incorrect and involves the medium reading the sitter psychically and obtaining psychic information about the sitter instead of comments from the deceased spirit.

However, I don't think this is always the case, as sometimes I believe spirits give communication or information about the sitter so that the medium knows they are with the correct person. That way they can identify who in the audience they are with. Another possible advantage of this is when the Spirit gives information about something going on in the sitter's life after they passed, serving to indicate to the sitter that the spirit is still with them, present, and knows what is going on in their life. Therefore, I think each situation has to be addressed individually, as there are no clearly black-and-white answers. Sometimes the medium may be off the track in obtaining psychic information, and sometimes the spirit may have a valid reason for wanting to give information about the sitter, his or her loved one, in order to direct the medium to the correct person or to indicate to the sitter that they are still present and aware of what is going on in their loved one's life.

Another somewhat controversial issue is whether or not the sitter should be allowed to ask the medium questions. I have heard one very good medium state that this is improper as it would involve conjecture, wasn't evidential, and couldn't be proven. He felt that anything asked could lead the medium down the wrong track and would not be evidential unless it was addressed by the Spirit first.

I feel very differently about this issue. I feel that the dialogue between the spirit and their loved one who remains living is a two-way street. I believe that readings are not only for giving evidence of survival after death, but are also important for resolving emotional issues, giving comfort, and for resolving conflicted or unfinished business. Let's say that there was unfinished business or regrets between the deceased loved one and the living loved one. Being able to ask questions of the loved one in spirit can help to resolve those issues or answer those unanswered questions that could now no longer be addressed in any other manner. I believe that readings are not just to give evidence of survival but to give comfort and answers to those who are bereaved.

* * *

The Amazing and Ingenious Ways Spirit Contacts Us

We have a relatively small Skype spirit circle and sometimes we feel we may run out of different spirits to bring through messages for practice. One of the ways that the spirits have overcome this problem is by a spirit bringing through different aspects of himself or different circumstances from different periods of his lifetime. When you have brought through a spirit once, this does not mean there is no new information to be brought through. A person's life contains many years of experience and exposure to different circumstances and people, changes of interests and environments, as well as modifications in personality. The same spirit can come through showing different aspects of himself or giving different information about his lifetime many times without ever repeating facts.

Another method Spirit uses to validate their messages is presenting the same identical statement or fact through several different mediums in different geographical areas who don't even know each other. My loved one in spirit did this for me from several mediums who repeated a phrase word for word.

Another example of this is when my mother communicated the same specific detail from my childhood through two different mediums in different places – she referenced an unusual and specific detail that multiple mediums would not likely have accidentally guessed. She referenced our work together hand-looming potholders when I was a child – a very specific uncommon experience we shared. I was astounded that one medium was able to bring through that unusual detail, let alone two.

Another method a spirit can use to clearly corroborate their presence is giving a bizarre, unusual or unique statement or fact through a medium that only the two of you knew. My friend, Harvey, got the message from spirit for me that two women were talking and saying, "Well, I guess we'll just have to bake an elephant cake." No one knew the memory associated with this statement except my deceased loved one and myself. Harvey thought this statement from spirit was so crazy that he thought it must be his imagination and wasn't even going to tell me. But guess what? That was the most evidential and intimate, personal detail that could have come through. It represented something only my loved one and I knew. Who would have guessed such a strange thing?

As a matter of fact, another young medium in another city, who didn't know my name or even know of me personally, and had never seen me before, summoned her courage and asked me, "Why is your mother giving me an elephant trunk?" WOW! Twice. How fantastic is that? That was confirmation to me that my mother in spirit now respects and is supporting my choices in a partner, and that meant a great deal to me.

Let's face it. It takes courage to stand in front of someone you don't know who is eager to get a message that may have a profound impact on their life, and also may be judging you, and say something to an outsider like that, that would surely sound nonsensical to you.

If I didn't already know Spirit is real, those unique messages from separate mediums who didn't know me from Adam would have given me absolute proof.

I was recently at a mediumship seminar with a dear friend of mine who is a medium and she gave me the most wonderful reading. I had just lost one of my dogs and was grieving the unexpected death. My friend, who was engaging in a teaching exercise and had to do the reading without seeing the sitter, didn't know that it was me.

She began by telling me that she had two children in spirit for me. They were both female and one passed as a teenager and the other at the age of 10. Both were wearing Halloween costumes and were dressed up as dogs. They were wagging their tails and she said it was so hard that she could feel it against her leg. They also had on matching necklaces (collars).

One mentioned Christmas as a holiday on which she was dressed up. I always took my dogs and had pictures taken of them at Christmas with the Santa Claus at the pet store to benefit the Humane Society. I have those pictures of my dogs all dressed up with Christmas stocking caps and bibs.

She said that when one passed she had a bellyache and was thankful that I was there with her at the end. This correlates with the manner in which my dog had recently died. I had driven a long way to be with her in the university veterinary ICU. She also added that the younger child had come into the world to comfort me for the loss of my older child. It is true that I got Holly after Belle passed to the spirit world. She said that when the younger one came to earth she knew that she would not be here long or have a long life. This was comforting to me, as I knew that her death could not have been prevented and I had done everything I could to try to help her. She mentioned that the older one was there to greet the younger one as she came across. This gave me comfort that she would be taken care of, and not be alone.

She said they loved me unconditionally and never wanted me to leave them. She also added, "I also feel that they gave Eskimo kisses with their noses." One said that she was naughty but that you loved her so much you didn't even notice it. This was true in the sense that long ago I had startled her while she was sleeping and she had bitten me on the nose.

All of this information matched my two dogs, and when my friend opened her eyes and saw me, she was astounded to find that the two "children" were actually my two dogs, whom I regarded as my four-legged children with tails.

If Spirit had given me that information as dogs it wouldn't have been nearly as evidential as getting it as children with all the facts matching and the medium totally unaware she was bringing through animals. Many of the readings I have gotten over the years are so precious to me that I keep them in my drawer as beautiful treasures I need only to review when I need uplifting.

* * *

Instructions for Opening Up

There are many ways we can open up or conduct readings. Some of the most effective I have found involve relaxing, placing tensions, worries, and daily concerns aside, to be re-addressed later and grounding myself. I then concentrate on breathing, visualizing the opening of my chakras like great, spinning, colored energy centers, and then visualize energy coming down from Spirit through my chakras. I see my own energy as a bright, white light, expanding and connecting me with the spirit world as I raise my level of consciousness and vibration. I imagine breathing positivity into the area of my heart and breathing out negativity, or anything that no longer serves my highest good, aware of each breath.

Simultaneously, I shift my awareness away from the material world to the spiritual world. Another medium I highly respect also suggests visualizing a column of white light going up from yourself to Source and asking the spirit communicator to step into that column of white light while communicating with you. That medium made me aware that worrying over the details of your communication and whether you are using your clairaudience, clairsentience, claircognizance or clairvoyance is not as important as strengthening the bond between yourself and the spirit.

Speaking of what are affectionately called the "clairs", she states that information from the spirit can be obtained through hearing, images, feeling, and knowingness, and that advanced mediums, although usually predominating in one sense or the other, utilize all modalities of communication naturally, without thinking about it. Using the "clairs" means saying, "I hear, I see, I feel, sense or know," while you are giving the reading.

One of the challenges for me is seeing the spirit objectively, standing by the sitter, rather than subjectively, with my eyes closed. Some mediums see them and where they're positioned by the sitter.

When bringing through a spirit, things that are important to include or address, are details regarding the spirit's personality and history with the sitter, identifying the relationship with the sitter, providing detailed evidence that the sitter will recognize, and then giving a message if there is one.

Knowing where you are pulled can be an advantage as a medium, versus "throwing out" information and then waiting to see where it fits. You may sense a pull or cord from your solar plexus extending to a sitter or particular section of the audience.

Several things that may be helpful when you are nervous about giving a reading are to remember that it's not about you, whether you succeed or fail, how you look to the audience, but about the spirit and the sitter, and their relationship. They are the clients.

I've been told that having an "attitude of gratitude" helps, and this keeps us humble and casts ego out. One medium said, when you become fearful, remind yourself, "I was born to do this." Even though your conscious mind may doubt this at times, on a soul level, you may have more conviction.

Gordon Higginson, a famous and accomplished British medium, condoned "sitting in the power," just establishing a contact with spirit regularly by relaxing and building the connection, before you seek specific information or messages. When building the power, extending love outward from yourself to expand and encompass others is a crucial facet.

One female medium said she had lived in an area that was remote, and had no one to practice with, and subsequently sat daily with spirit to develop a connection, despite not having other people to help her progress.

Trust is also essential. Do not let your conscious mind filter out or add to the messages you receive. Do not let your opinions and beliefs color the message of the spirit. Remember that they are a distinct individual with their own unique viewpoint and convictions.

Also, do not let your conscious mind embellish the message. I've had a professional medium do this in a message for me, expanding beyond the message that my aunt was an avid gardener to making her a horticulturalist, which she wasn't.

Another young medium in training gave me a message of my loved one carrying a gun, but didn't stop there. She made him into a hunter, which he wasn't. He had carried a gun in the service. So don't let your own mind interpret the data coming through and throw a wrong spin on it. To quote a famous medium, just "Give what you get."

* * *

MAKING RAINBOWS

Tips I have learned for enhancing mediumship readings

As a medium, you can give a sitter many facts regarding their deceased loved one, but it is equally, if not more important to bring through the essence or personality of their loved one, to bring forth corroboration of the relationship and the memories between the sitter and their deceased loved one. In essence, you are bringing the loved one alive by doing this. You are re-creating their personality and individual characteristics, being their voice, and bringing them into the room. You are an actor or actress, portraying them, allowing them to live again through you for their loved one to see them and hear them.

Different mediums have different names for this process. Some call it blending, allowing the spirit to overlay you, or even allowing the spirit to step into your auric field temporarily. This just means allowing the spirit to come close to you, overshadow you, and make you see, hear, and feel what they saw, heard, and felt. It is a temporary blending or merging of your two energy fields. This is not something to be feared as long as you establish ground rules and are working "at the vibration of love." It may not be surprising when there is a strong blending for the medium to express him or herself in language the deceased loved one used, or even to display some of their mannerisms.

I have a friend who has inexplicably been influenced to wear particular clothing or buy flowers before a reading, only to find out those were the flowers the sitter's loved one preferred or the clothing was similar to that the loved one used to wear. In fact, my friend has also had an unexplained urge to mention the name of her own relative or one of their interests, later finding out that the sitter had a relative with that same name and interest. So Spirit can use information from the medium's life to get them to mention something that will be relevant to the sitter and his or her deceased loved one.

Mediums also describe the interaction with spirit as facilitated by a shift in consciousness or awareness from the lower earthly vibration to the higher spiritual vibration. In part, this involves becoming passive or stilling the mind so that you can hear the spirit world speak or impress you with their ideas, images, and feelings. It also involves a receptiveness facilitated by strong desire on both sides and a conscious shift of your attention or focus to the spirit plane or level of vibration. Being peaceful, joyous, anticipating, trusting, and positive facilitate the communication. It can be accompanied by a sense of exhilaration and euphoria.

Some mediums refer to it as tapping into the power of BIG LOVE. This means a higher sense of empathy with all other souls, accompanied by thankfulness and expansive love for all others. Vanora, a medium at Hollister Rand's recent seminar, described the change in brain waves of mediums linking with spirit as demonstrating measurable gamma waves. She states that activating your heart chakra, thinking of someone you love deeply, and then extending that love to others, feeling your soul or essence as a white light expanding, helps induce a state of unification, and jump starts our production of gamma brain waves. Wishing health, happiness, and healing for others facilitates this state of larger consciousness.

She also suggested that we connect with spirit by setting our intention to match the higher vibrational frequencies of violet, gold, or white. For those who had trepidation, and were fearful of making mistakes, she recommended regarding every stumble as taking you one step closer to achieving your goals. My Irish grandmother, after whom I'm named, also a medium, said, "Every knock is a boost."

Using symbols is another way of obtaining information from spirit faster. Working mediums who need to obtain information fast often use symbols. Each medium has his or her unique symbols, but whatever you use, you need to work the system out with spirit so they can take advantage of the shorthand. Devising symbols that can designate gender, means of death – chronic illness, acute illness, accident, murder, or suicide can be helpful. Creating ways of determining relationship to the sitter, such as friend, or position in family, can also be helpful. Some spirits I see more clearly and others I can hear. Having symbols or set methods can definitely speed up the process.

At a recent seminar we were given names of well-known people and places which a group of six of us drew from a basket. Each group got one name, which was hidden to us and we took turns saying the first image or thing that popped into our minds. I decided not to worry about the results, but to wait until I heard or saw something and just give it no matter how crazy it might seem. I first got the image of two hands praying; then I heard applause, and finally got the sense of two broken hearts. When the name was finally revealed, we had Whitney Houston. I knew she had come from a religious background and gospel music. Applause was certainly appropriate to her life as a performer. The two broken hearts may have represented hers and her daughter's at her death. I feel that just getting out of the way and not letting my reasoning mind interfere with what I got and said helped me to get appropriate information.

Speaking of synchronicities, this is one that stands out in my mind. Two weeks after I lost my dog I got a reading from a medium at a seminar which was done "blind", without her seeing me, the sitter. She brought through my two deceased dogs with a plethora of accurate details, thinking they were my two children. Two weeks after that, at another seminar, a medium and participant was taking orb pictures and my dog's head is clearly seen in the picture. Before she even knew I had lost a dog, as she reviewed the picture on her camera, she asked me, "Did you lose an animal, because I'm seeing an animal's face in this orb?" I showed her a picture of that dog on my cell phone, which matched the face in the orb. Later that same day a different medium accurately described three of my prior dogs, describing details associated with each accurately, including their size and color, the place I was living when I got them, a Christmas connection with one, who was a Christmas present, and the color of the collar of the last one. But there's more. I had to pick a card unseen from a deck and the medium opposite me gave me a reading based on the card. Well, there was a little dog on the bottom of the card dwarfed by the main image, but the medium's eyes go right to it and she starts talking about the dog connection.

How's that for synchronicities? I'm impressed.

50

Memorable Messages

THERE ARE SOME messages you get from spirit that have a direct bearing on your present personal life situation, but also have a universal relevance. One such message from my mother came through for me in a recent spirit circle.

I was a little discouraged about the amount of work I was doing as well as about a faux pas I had committed recently, which had caused a temporary setback in a personal relationship.

First the medium gave me many details to corroborate who was speaking to me. She provided many evidential details specific to my mother and our history, such as hanging clothes and women's slips on a clothes line (my mother washed many clothes by hand and frequently hung them on clothes lines and she also wore slips), a small boat next to a dock (I have a picture of it – my parents' boat- that I was recently looking at), a woven hand loomed potholder (yes, I made those with my mother when I was a child), and a specific shuffling dance my mother did (actually we did it together frequently when I was young). These were very unique evidential details that came through among many others, and every detail in this particular reading was right-on accurate.

At the end of the reading came the message. The medium described my mother taking some food out of the oven and it had fallen or partially collapsed. It was something like a soufflé. She said this was a metaphor conveying the message that things can't always be perfect as we would like them to be, but even when they're not, they can still be "incredibly good".

That message made me feel so much better about my life right now and the mistakes I sometimes make. I realized that sometimes my expectations can be high and I am somewhat obsessive compulsive, disappointing myself and others. But when I look at it with that new perspective she conveyed, I can truthfully say, sometimes stuff happens, but yes, things are still incredibly good.

Another message that came through was one a friend related to me from a seminar she had just attended in Virginia Beach with internationally acclaimed medium Robert Brown. I had signed up to go, but caught a severe bronchitis from a co-worker and ended up in the hospital, missing the conference. My friend told me about the following message.

Robert was demonstrating ethical mediumship and the importance of giving accurate messages and he had some attendees come up front, having several "play" act as sitters and one as the medium. My friend was called upon to play the medium. It was a simulation or demonstration. As my friend started to open her mouth to give a made up example, to her surprise, a real spirit started coming through and speaking.

The spirit essentially said she was so grateful for the chance to speak to and comfort her loved ones, she didn't mind if the messages weren't 100% perfect or if the medium got it not quite exact all the time. She was just so thankful to be able to reach out and connect with her loved ones from the other dimension.

Messages given at the vibration of love from spirit should be positive, comforting, helpful, and healing. People should feel better at the end of a reading. One saying that I like is from the medium, Hollister Rand, who said that hope allows us to write a different end to our story. I can vouch for the truth of that saying from my own personal experience of love, lost and found.

This was a message I didn't expect, and so poignant. It touched my heart. I thought, what a miracle it seems to be, to be able to hear our deceased loved ones, and how beautiful to know they're alive and well, that they love us, and we can still be in touch, even if the process isn't perfect, if the medium gets something wrong sometimes or says something in a different way.

Who is always 100% accurate or perfect in their work in this material world? Who has never made a mistake? How much more so is that true when trying to get spirit messages from another world into the human brain? I think what I have gotten, though sometimes imperfect, is precious, cherished, treasured, and inexpressibly important to the healing of my heart.

So many incredible details have come through from spirit. My loved one has corroborated his presence with many private details of our lives. He has also given me messages and "scenarios" that display his wonderful, quirky sense of humor – like one about the time I decided to cook him an elaborate, gourmet meal. The medium said, "He's showing me you in the kitchen and an immaculately set table. Now I'm seeing you frantic and smoke pouring out of the oven." No one else knew about this little incident. Jig's up.

Later he sent me a funny scenario – a bunch of elaborate images – which, as a disclaimer, are completely untrue and all in fun. He showed me the following images. I was in a kitchen, hosting my own show, "Kitchen Disasters." As I got ready to add the eggs to a bowl, they slid off the counter top onto the floor. As I stepped back, I slid on the eggs and fell on my rear. Undaunted, I got up and turned on the MixMaster, but it was on high, and little clots of dough were flying up and sticking on the ceiling. Meanwhile, the smoke alarm went off and I ran to the stove where smoke was billowing out. As I opened the door, my apron caught on fire, and I said, "Oh, _ _ _ _", as the firemen dowsed everything with their hoses, and ingredients went flying off the counters. Then an ambulance pulls up and the medics carry the turkey out on a stretcher with its legs sticking up. Then the phone rings and it's a weight loss program asking me to cook for its patrons. My partner gets on a talking scale, that says, "98 pounds and counting down." So, as a present, he enrolls me in a cooking class, "Remedial Cooking" and I am concentrating on the first lesson, "How to Boil Water." My partner's testimony to my cooking? "Oh, no."

Now I'm not really that bad, am I? I don't think so. Well, maybe. Ok, Ok, I admit it.

My partner has also given me incredibly romantic, treasured messages. Through other mediums, he has given me Phil Collins' song, "Dance into the Light", and Paul McCartney's song, "My Love". Recently he showed the medium, Karuna, a long scroll that he unwrapped, and he was writing in it. This refers to vows we placed in the Akashic records after he passed, and is a beautiful and evidential message and testimony to our mutual commitment. I'm the luckiest lady in the world to have his love. I once heard a comment from spirit, "You'll be the happiest couple in Heaven. But every couple in Heaven feels that they're the happiest."

51

Planning Mistakes

ARE WE AWARE of the problems we will encounter on earth or the mistakes we will make before we come to earth?

My guide:

We are aware before we come to earth what our challenges and problems are going to be. We are aware of what our most likely issues and errors will be, because we are aware of our weaknesses and obstacles before we come to earth. We are aware of what our difficulties will be, and what we will experience if we overcome them or succumb to them. We know what our biggest problems will be, and we plan some for the enlightenment and awareness of ourselves and others by learning what the results will be, the ramifications, depending on how we address, that is, solve or fail to solve, those problems. We may even plan certain circumstances with likely failures or likely difficult or problematic outcomes, so that we and other others involved learn from the negative results.

We are learning by experience, both negative and positive, about how to address problems in the most positive and efficacious manner, and about the results of our weaknesses and imperfect behavior on ourselves and on others.

By experiencing and attempting to deal with the negative, we are challenged and grow as souls in the knowledge of the outcome of our behavior, both negative and positive, on ourselves and others.

By negative experience, we attempt to adjust our behavior to be less harmful to ourselves and others. For example, we may learn from a negative parental experience to be a better parent ourselves, or by being an addict, to gain strength so as not to harm or injure ourselves and others.

By learning the effects of our wrongs on ourselves and others, we inch forward in learning, to control ourselves and cope with others in a more productive manner as much as possible. Only by falling and crawling do we learn to stand and walk.

Do we plan our problems and the mistakes we will make before we come to earth? Is it possible to plan a flaw that we or others will learn from?

Harvey's guides:

No, not directly. We planned a general path and the problems are usually from the situations we contact on earth. It's from the different interactions with other souls. No, we don't plan mistakes.

52

Near Death Experiences

WHY THE DICHOTOMY between some people who have had near death experiences and see God as a loving, intelligent spirit, and others who are channeled describing God as a force without "personality", a "blind force"?

How is it possible that some channeled works about the other side report spirits as saying there is a higher power but nothing we would describe as a Spirit, while others infer the presence of an intelligent God, and still others, particularly those who have had near death experiences, describe personal interactions with God? What is the real truth? In any case, with so many differing testimonies, we won't know definitively until we, ourselves, make the transition.

From the understanding I have been given of the afterlife, those on the other side know there is a creator or supreme being, but those I have contacted have not told me they saw, spoke with, or witnessed God personally. Just the fact that we survive death, that we cross over to the other side with our consciousness and personality intact, should be enough to make us believe in a greater source than ourselves and a greater plan for existence. It seems that those who pass over do not have all knowledge, and that there are more advanced levels of spirit consciousness that are more aware of the ultimate truth. Until we reach those levels, our faith and conviction, the answer we find, must lie within our own soul.

On the television show, "The Last Goodbye", medium Rebecca Rosen sees a son who was murdered send a spirit who was one of his soul connections to be his former mother's new son. So personalities and individualities still persist.

Why is it that some individuals who have had near death experiences, such as Freddy, on "Project Afterlife", say that all thoughts of earth and human thoughts of loved ones and family were erased, and some souls didn't want to come back to earth, while others say that they see deceased relatives who wanted them to stay in the afterlife but that they wanted to return to earth because of their family, children, husband, wife, or loved ones?

I believe this depends on the person, their values, priorities, the strength of their connections with loved ones left behind, and the purpose of their near death experience. Some are apparently given a choice of whether to stay or return, and if their path didn't call for them to die, their choice appears to be dependent upon their desire for completion of a physical life and the strength of the links with those left behind.

Many who had near death experiences stated that they spoke with God or Jesus, and some of the relatives on earth also claimed to have heard God speak to them regarding their deceased loved one. Some children who are the possible subjects of reincarnation are reported as saying that they died before and God sent them right back to earth to be reborn.

Others who purport to have seen the afterlife and returned, stated that they saw the prayers as energy going directly to God. One wife whose husband had a near death experience stated that positive thought was extremely important in facilitating his return from death, as well as in causing desirable outcomes in their earth lives.

Some of the lessons people felt they learned from their near death experiences included saying you're sorry quickly, forgiving quickly and being quick to love.

Also, why is it true that some people return to earth from their near death experience, and their relatives' and love ones' prayers are answered, while others pray fervently but still lose their loved ones to death? I was told by my guide that those were people whose near death experiences had a purpose. Some are told, "You have to go back, it's not your time," and others are given a choice. Each situation is different, and if all of our prayers were answered, no one would ever die. But we all know death for humans is inevitable.

It appears that many near death experiences are for the edification of the individual, whose life may have been on the wrong track, or for the benefit to loved ones and others whose lives they might touch. Given that there appears to be a purpose in many near death experiences, that may explain why each individual experiences something different that correlates with their belief system or is comforting. Think of it. Who would you turn to for help if you needed it? A loved one, someone trusted, a religious figure you may have believed in, or perhaps God, himself?

I'm sure that those who have near death experiences usually encounter others they are familiar with, who comfort them. In the case of negative near death experiences in which some describe seeing "Hell" or dire circumstances, many of these encounters seem to be for the purpose of serving a warning, or helping the individual to get his or her life re-oriented in a positive direction.

53

Negative Levels – Punishment?

WHAT ARE THE lower realms like?

My guide:

The lower realm is filled with others like themselves and they are unhappy because of their deeds. With their cumulative negative energy there is very little light and uplifting atmosphere. They are mental prisoners to their own past deeds and feel the suffering they have caused others. It is a denser, less joyous atmosphere and their confinement to this lower energy with others like themselves is a punishment in itself.

The recrimination of their thoughts and deeds feels like a dense fog and prevents them from experiencing the joy of more developed levels and they, through their words, thoughts, and deeds, have cut themselves off from God or divine joy, so to speak, as one alienated who must redeem himself through learning, effort, change, love, and service.

What happens to those who have lived a negative life and harmed others when they pass into the afterlife?

My guide:

Each goes to his own environment that is apropos to his development. Souls are sifted or divided, separated by their capabilities and level of understanding, as students can be divided into basic, regular, and honors groups.

They have some that are not capable of understanding what others can, so they don't occupy the same dimension. Souls that are more negative are stuck in an atmosphere of their own quality. The predominant mood or temper of their thoughts and emotions places them in an environment of like or similar emotions, and creates their surroundings and ambient reality.

There are souls who will help them progress, but this can only happen if they are amenable to it or desire it, and then they will draw the help to themselves and can move into lighter, brighter, and happier, more palatable atmospheres and conditions.

We draw the reality to us that our thoughts, ideas, and judgments dictate. That's why they say that we are the judge and jury. We judge ourselves, so to speak.

The Bible refers to the wheat growing up with the tares, but after death, the wheat is separated from the chaff. This could refer to the separation by moral development in the afterlife.

What happens to serial killers and people who practice evil when they cross over? Are they punished? Are they in the same place as "good" people?

Harvey's guides:

They enter in at the lowest level possible. On the earth plane, it's called "purgatory" and they stay there as long as necessary before they can rise to the level of enlightenment. It's a learning experience, but someone who does good progresses quickly.

There are many parallel levels at entry – the life you live determines where you go to. It's called the book of life, which often is currently called the Akashic records. Everything is recorded in the book of life.

Depending on your history, even a killer may have a family. It depends on them whether they want to associate with him. When people love one another it is not likely that they will be separated. You will be greeted by someone you love or want to see, which is determined by you at the earliest sign of death, and you will be with that person on the other side. You may be with one person or a dozen.

MAKING RAINBOWS

What happens to people who lived negative and malicious lives when they pass over? Where do they go?

Harvey's guides:

They may have been seeing what they feared on the earth plane. What they may be seeing was what was in their mind when they performed the negative deeds. It is a wake-up call. They're getting a second chance. Don't screw it up.

They go to an entry-level and usually stay there much longer than those who live an exemplary life. They have to unlearn some of the things and they have to pay for misdeeds.

* * *

I had a close relative, now deceased, whose friend, who had done some negative and harmful things to others in his lifetime, came to him in a dream after he died and indicated that he was in a bad place but that soon he would be able to improve things and be in a better place that was "right over there." Where was he?

Harvey's guides:

He was reliving what he did. When they open the book of life, the Akashic records, and read, he was reliving what he did.

Everyone comes to the lower levels. No one goes straight to the top. He has to go through a healing first. He knew there was a place that was better. Someone who hurt someone unintentionally doesn't necessarily go there. Someone who lived his life with malice stays there quite a while. It's a painful dark place. Try to do some good. Leave a path behind you. It's like earning points. Pay it forward. Everyone should do something without having their hand out for a return.

54

Plans For Negativity

DO SPIRITS EVER plan to do negative things in order for others to learn lessons?

My guide:

They can as long as other spirits involved are in agreement.

Do we know what our mistakes will be before we come to earth?

My guide:

Based upon our challenges and the awareness of what our personal weaknesses are, we can predict what our mistakes are likely to be if make them.

55

Spiritual Oneness

IDEAS ARE NOT owned by anyone. They may be shared ideas, expressed by anyone. Just so, reality and love are shared.

Isn't it wonderful to be alive when you share that with someone, even if they have crossed the threshold into the afterlife? That someone is alive, too, just without a physical body as we know it, and we are connecting, sharing, and communicating. In the deepest sense we can be one – as in the Bible it says the husband and wife become one. It is a great mystery. Their thoughts, desires, hopes, and happiness become united with ours on a common path.

That bridge can be maintained by two loving souls in the harmony and love of spiritual partnership. It is the union behind the shell of the body that is the lasting one. Some have found that eternal bond. They are co-mingling, entangled, part of one another, two comprising a greater whole. They have forged their destinies together.

56

Other Comments

THER COMMENTS

Harvey's guides:

God doesn't have a gender. God can be anything or all things. There's also no prejudice on the other side. A lot of things that separate us on earth don't exist on the other side. When you cross over to spirit, spirit is pure.

Since spirits don't have physical bodies, per se, how is it that some mediums refer to spirits eating?

Medium Hollister Rand, in her recent newsletter, mentions a young spirit who says that she can eat whatever she wants in Heaven without gaining weight. Another refers to preparing a Thanksgiving dinner for the newcomers, and yet another who passed from anorexia says she now enjoys food. My guide and loved one gave me a message through another medium, A. J. Barrera, that he still loves eating on the other side.

They are not eating physically as we know it, digesting or processing food with a physical body, but are rather re-creating the experience of eating with their thoughts. The act and sensation are rather simulated and feel real although they do not exist in a "physical sense".

Don't dreams and hallucinations feel real? Although our sensory apparatus in the physical world allows us to interact with our environment and process physical information, the sensations of eating, seeing, touching, feeling, and hearing are actually perceived by the mind. They are apprehended and processed by the mind, only transmitted to the mind as electrical signals by the nerves. The thought is what is "real" to us, even when we are in the physical body.

Therefore, the thought of eating, sex, or any other physical activity known to us can be re-created or experienced by us on the other side, making the experience feel as real to the participating soul as the physical act is to us. The reality doesn't have to come by means of a physical body and sensory system, but is directly produced and experienced by the mind. The mind creates the experience, which is reproduced and felt as realistically as it would have been on earth. John Scott, in his book, "As One Ghost to Another", and Frederic Myers, purportedly channeled in Geraldine Cummins' book, "Beyond Human Personality", state that, with their newfound and enhanced powers, spirits can re-create an experience such as eating or sex, feeling for all practical purposes that they are enjoying the same act that they did on earth.

Other comments

My Guide:

When people return to the other side they see things in a different light. The blinders of the earth perception come off. They process information and compare it to what they have learned in other lives. They are free from the prejudices and personal agendas of the human existence and condition,, and see things in a truer light. They don't have an axe to grind. It is both freeing and revealing when the presumptions that cloud our perception vanish away. It truly is an awakening or rebirth. Although retaining our individuality and personality, in a sense, with our new awareness, we become new creatures.

57

Experiencing the Paranormal

WHEN WE FEEL and see something paranormal, whether or not it is momentarily material (can be touched, heard, and seen) or is an illusion planted in our mind, that seems real to us, in either case it is for all practical purposes "real" to us, whether or not it is truly material or permanent. Since nothing material is in the same state permanently, if it can be recreated, re-enacted, and experienced, it is nevertheless real to us. The actor, Dick Van Patten, described his experience with a spirit in the physical realm on Celebrity Ghost Stories episode, "Don't Drink the Water".

How an image, feeling, or communication gets into our mind, whether through the physical senses, or through the more insubstantial spirit communication, it is nevertheless real to the observer and participant.

58

Letting Go of the Past

EMERGING FROM THE painful past is like awakening from a long, bad dream. It becomes a distant memory, a recollection that no longer causes pain in the present tense.

When you let go of the painful past, you no longer empower it to enslave you or harm your present life. You no longer continue to suffer from something in the present that caused you to suffer in the past.

Why should you let it have authority over you? If you made a mistake or someone else harmed you, don't allow them or yourself to continue harming you by repeating the same mistakes or reliving the painful scenario.

I, myself, had so much trouble letting go of the woulda, shoulda, coulda. I let this terrible trio cause me to experience continued depression, threaten my current relationships, and cause me to waste so much precious time that could have been better spent.

If you have a big demon of the past lurking above you, do not let it slay you. Vanquish it instead by refusing to give it power, and by saying, I learned from those negative experiences and I will not repeat them again. I am now free from them. I no longer have to suffer hurt from them, because that's in the past. I am free to move on and live a happier and better life with those I love.

Cut the umbilical cord on the negative experiences of the past and make them vanish like shadows in the night. Replace them with happier and better experiences commandeered by your newly gained wisdom.

One spirit father, communicating to his son on "The Long Island Medium", wisely said, "Don't think of them as mistakes. Think of them as lessons learned."

59

What Are Our Paths?

Rebecca Rosen, the medium from the television series, "The Last Goodbye", commented in a reading, "It was not your job to fix him. That was his path."

I begin to question, when someone becomes a drug addict and dies in the gutter of an overdose, is that their path? Did they decide in the afterlife that this is how they will end their life?

It didn't make sense to me that spirits would choose such disasters and tragedies to "meet their fate". I reasoned that our path is probably a set of general circumstances and relationships that we will encounter with certain obstacles planned, but yet we can meet those obstacles with free will and choices, so we can produce different outcomes based upon our behavior.

Our path is a general direction we chose before we came to earth for purposes of learning and overcoming obstacles, for choosing wisely, making better decisions for the welfare of all, for taking as much positive from a negative situation as possible, for acting in faith and producing positive results. But the path is not set in stone. We can change it and make it better or worse.

We can succumb or overcome. It is the triumph of the spirit over the physical roadblocks that we seek.

60

Retention of Personality

My guide states:

We lose the outside physical and cultural manifestations of our personality, but the core personality, our individuality, remains.

We are all one in spirit, not in personality.

A paranormal investigator team, the McKinney's, on an episode of the television program, "Alaska Haunting", made the statement, "We've had many instances where we've discovered that whatever characteristics a person had in their life follow them over into the afterlife."

My loved one and guide has said:

I'm the same person I was on earth, only a little more kind, loving, and caring.

61

Planes

Planes or levels of spirit life correspond with spiritual development and vibrational level.

Much as the electromagnetic spectrum exists simultaneously all around us but can only be perceived if the receiver is attuned to it, as dogs can hear a different portion of the audible spectrum that humans can't, and we now have cameras that can capture the portion of the light spectrum corresponding with ultraviolet, spiritual levels can coexist in the same geographical space but can be separated or distinct by vibration, and perceived only by those attuned to them.

This explains that spiritual planes do not have to be geographically distinct but can be vibrationally distinct, effectively limiting them to those who are attuned to them.

A message I received through another medium from my loved one in spirit and others I received from Harvey's guides indicate that spirits are grouped by level of vibration that correlates with development, and another medium, E., gave me the message that like-minded spirits with similar views and preferences are more inclined to remain together. Many texts state that progressing to advanced levels generally reduces contact with those on earth. In Anthony Borgia's book, "Life in the World Unseen", Monsignor Hugh Benson purportedly channels that a spirit may choose to remain on a particular level rather than advance in order to remain with a loved one. Some travel between levels is described in many books for purposes of learning, helping, or teaching.

62

Personal Preference and the Law of Like Attraction

I HAVE ALWAYS HEARD that life on the other side is lived in the atmosphere of love. It is said that spirits are more loving. In an atmosphere of transparency, where thoughts are directly communicated, souls become more considerate of others' feelings. Without the negative situations and acts that proliferate on the earth, there is greater harmony. Can you imagine a world where there is no poverty, hunger, violence, abuse, prejudice, and exploitation? On the other side, there is reportedly less selfishness, more concern for the welfare of others. But one book, "The Awakening Letters, volume 2", by Cynthia Sandys, states that there is an impersonal Godly love as well as a personal love.

This means that we can love all other souls in a godly way, without judgment, and with love for their well-being and progress. The personal love is expressed in the law of like attraction. If we think of our friends or families, we recognize that there are some people we are closer to than others. There are some people we chose not to form a friendship with, and others that become closest friends. There are some relatives we are not close to and others with whom we have a deep and loving relationship. This is also true on the other side. Not only do we not know all souls on the other side, it would not be possible to spend equal amounts of time and have equally close relationships with all of the infinite number of souls in existence. I am told that on the other side we gravitate to our own level of development and to like minded souls with similar goals, desires, and natures.

Imagine this. If all of the bad things were removed from us and we were more considerate, kind, and caring; if no one actively exercised harm toward another; if all our bad characteristics were removed and we became nicer, there would be much more love in general, one for another.

But with all of the bad removed, with nicer and kinder behavior, unless our individual personalities, outlooks, interests, desires, and characteristics were eliminated, we would still have varying degrees of greater and lesser compatibility, affinity, sympathy, and closeness. We would still have greater and lesser individual preferences and loves for one another. Diane, communicating in Jeffrey Mark's book, "The Afterlife Interviews, volume 1", states that "The love you have for everyone is in the sense of servicing them on their journeys." Those who are of the same vibration, or on the same frequency or journey remain together.

Amidst the greater consideration and love, there would still be some stronger individual bonds unless our personalities, outlooks, opinions, interests, preferences, and temperaments were erased. However kind and loving we may be, as long as we are different individuals, there will be a stronger compatibility and individual love between some than others. This fact explains a communication from the spirit group Silver as communicated through my medium friend, Karuna, in answer to my question as to whether there are unions, pairings, or eternal love and companionships on the other side. They communicated, "There are some spirits who have been together for eons and eons."

My loved one and guide states, "Although there is a greater godly love, due to our individuality and personalities, some are more intimately connected than others."

No relationship is ideal because we are not perfect, but if two souls are compatible, love, accept, discuss issues, compromise, forgive, help, support, and appreciate one another, I believe a love relationship can be eternal.

63

Pretensions

AT A RECENT conference one exercise we were given was to write a letter from the other side from a deceased loved one to a living loved one. I received a beautiful letter that also gave me a piece of information. My loved one said that on the other side the pretensions fall away. The masks come off and you cannot hide who you truly are. You are known and your thoughts and deeds are transparent. Your true nature, feelings, and thoughts are revealed. The earthly deceptions are gone and you are naked so to speak.

This may be shocking for those who have worn a "costume" all their lives, but ultimately, how refreshing to know one another for who we really are, no longer deceived by appearances.

This openness will only be a problem for those who have something to hide.

64

Addressing Problems

THE MISTAKE IN life is thinking that with positive thought and intention you can fix everything in your life and make it right. That is an illusion that is sold to the public like dangling a carrot in front of them that's unreachable. Most of us want that perfect husband, family, job, talent, house, possession, etc.

Positive thinking doesn't mean you will get everything ideal and perfect.

What if your life's lesson was to die young of that disease? Then positive thinking won't prevent it. It is a mistake to buy into the mindset that you can cure all problems or make your life perfect by positive thinking.

Of course, your attitude will help, and govern your behavior, help your circumstances, but just realize that the fairytale ending may have a strong dose of reality, not all fantasy, and you may have to work to do the best you can, as in the phrase, "This is as good as it gets."

As long as we have flaws and other people have flaws, and circumstances have flaws, we are likely to be disappointed if we set too high a standard and expectation. Make the real your ideal before you attempt to find the ideal and escape or avoid the real.

Accept that little measure of imperfection and work with what you've got to improve it. You will probably be happiest if you don't have unrealistic expectations. If what you're thinking about creates a change in your behavior and produces a better outcome, you have a winner.

65

Personal Proof

THERE ARE PEOPLE who say all that they cannot see with their own eyes, touch, feel through the senses, is not real. All that cannot be proven with instruments doesn't exist.

I grant you that, although there are those who believe in what they can't see, seeing truly is believing. That old commercial "Only your hairdresser knows for sure" has an element of truth. After all, if experience is irrelevant, why do we need to come to the earth to experience things?

It has been stated in the mediumship literature that as souls, we may intellectually be aware of something, but until we have experienced it ourselves, we never fully know it. Can a woman who has never had a child fully know the pain of childbirth? We can draw analogies for ourselves, but we must experience it to completely understand it.

That's why all the words I put on paper of what I have personally experienced may be a signpost, but they will never replace the knowing you will have by experiencing it yourselves.

Is it for you? Do you want it? I don't know. Only you have those answers, along with the Source of all life. I can only tell what I know and encourage you to seek it yourself within the boundaries of prayer and divine protection.

When you know and experience it for yourself, no one will have to tell you it's real. You'll know it in your heart.

66

God Given Purpose

Do we each have a specific God-given intent or mission for our existence?

My guide:

We each have a God-given identity, purpose and direction. We are not identical when we emerge from Source. We are each unique with a mission specific to our soul. The mission given to us is appropriate to our identity, character, and interests.

Does each of us have a God-given purpose as well as individual lessons we need to learn in each lifetime?

Harvey's guides:

Our mission is contingent on the needs of the earth plane at that time. We are not given a script. We're given a direction. Our mission changes as their needs change. You both learn and teach at the same time.

That plan will be the feedback from what we learn and teach on earth. Yes. We have a specific direction. But specific actions, no.

67

Making Rainbows

A FRIEND OF MINE who is a medium is the medium and moderator of her own radio shows, and hosts many other mediums as guests. One recent guest was a medium from the Arthur Findlay College of Mediumship in England. His name is Matthew Smith.

My friend asked me to submit some questions to her as he was going to go into trance on the show, and spirits would speak through him and answer the questions. I was delighted to do this, as I took the same questions and asked them of my guide and my friend, Harvey's, guides. It was enlightening to compare the answers to the same questions, and this demonstrates the differences of opinions among spirits, indicating that we do not become robots or omniscient when we die, as spirit answers differ. This indicates that we remain unique individuals after we die.

One comment by Matthew Smith was of particular interest to me. He spontaneously commented at the end of the program, they are sending me a comment, an idea, or thought which just

— 212 —

MAKING RAINBOWS

"popped into my mind." "Don't chase rainbows, make them. This statement is intended for one or more of my listeners."

I immediately put two and two together and connected with that comment. Recently, in one of our spirit or development circles, a loved one and guide said to me, "You are always chasing rainbows," meaning that I was preoccupied with wanting to change the mistakes I made in the past and relive my life in a different way. Well, we obviously can't go back and "undo" what was done, as that would change everyone else's lives as well as our own. But the desire to complete things that were unfulfilled in my lifetime was strong.

The comment hit home. It was meant for me to recognize that I shouldn't expend so much energy lamenting what I didn't do, that I wish I had done, but rather to move those regrets into the present tense and make those rainbows now that I failed to make in the past. Fix the mistakes, not by erasing them but by not making them again, by sculpting the life I wanted and didn't have now, by making them now into the life I wish I had in the past but didn't.

It was a comment that it isn't too late to live what I so deeply desire and didn't finish in my previous life. All is not lost. Make it now, bring it into being or fruition if you failed to do so in the past. That is what mistakes are for – to help you live a better life and to create a better reality, not to repeat them.

Sometimes, if we cannot fulfill that reality in this world, we can fulfill it on the other side.

A spirit came through Theresa Caputo, the Long Island Medium, and made a statement I liked. What was intended for someone else I learned from. A deceased father came through to speak to his son, who had regrets about some mistakes he had made in his life. The father said "Don't look at them as mistakes, but as lessons learned."

I thought that was the epitome of taking something negative and making it positive. Don't see the failure in what you did wrong, but the overcoming, the transformation that will enable you to make better choices now and in the future.

68

Communication – Readings From Living People

How is it that sometimes mediums can bring through a person who isn't dead?

I have been told that, since we are all energy, that energy can be tuned into or read whether we are alive or dead. If the medium is having a dialogue with that soul or getting answers from them directly, it is presumed that they are dead or astrally out of their body.

I was told that that is why psychic detectives can read energy of both living and dead individuals, but are most often able to "feel" or discriminate whether a person is alive or dead.

Some mediums have also brought through information from a person who was in a coma or had Alzheimer's disease. It was explained to me that with those in altered mental states, the spirit may be transiently outside of the body, and as such, able to communicate independent of the brain.

69

Spirit Recognition

How do we recognize each other on the other side? Do we have a unique identifier?

On earth there are many ways we can be identified. We have names that are sound combinations when spoken and visual combinations when written. We are recognized by sight or by our unique physical appearance. Animals can identify us by scent or smell. We can identify a food by taste. Sometimes we can identify a writer or author by his style of syntax, particular words chosen, or ideas expressed.

That is how literary scholars attempted to identify the authorship of several disputed works as belonging to either Sir Francis Bacon or William Shakespeare.

We each have a unique emotional makeup and thought patterns or ideas. In the other world they say thoughts and feelings are transparent, so perhaps we could identify each other by these. On earth there was a TV show once where a man would try to identify his wife while blindfolded by touching her.

On the other side, since we don't have physical bodies, we wouldn't have a scent, although we could probably "manufacture" an odor like ghosts have been known to do. We don't have a set physical appearance, so we obviously couldn't use that. We don't always use speech, so a name or sound wouldn't always be applicable.

Imagine a spirit known by the signature sound of aahooogah, or the Jaws theme, the Twilight Zone theme, or the Lone Ranger theme.

What remains consistent and characteristic? Our emotions, our thoughts do. So are we identified by these, or do we have a particular vibration that is unique from all others? Is it intuition, like when you know who's calling before you answer the phone?

How do we know each other on earth? We know each other with set appearances, spoken words, a set form to touch, or a particular scent. We can also be identified by fingerprints or DNA on earth. What identifies us on the other side?

My guide gave me a humorous image of him recognizing me on the other side with my hair sticking out off my head like I had just touched a Tesla coil, been electrocuted, or was the bride of Frankenstein. Guess what? I just recognized him by his sense of humor.

My medium friend, Karuna, describes it as recognizing a spirit by its unique energy, which of course could translate into vibration. She can recognize different spirits by feeling their unique energy. This can mean she has a "receiver" built in that picks up their unique "ethos" or personality – which includes their prevailing mood, their unique outlook, likes and dislikes, characteristic opinions, or temperament, their preferences, their ideas and thoughts, their interests and their unique abilities, their attitudes, their desires.

However, it should also be noted that for us on earth recognizing the unique spirit energy must also be dependent on the spirit being willing to convey their energy, because several times my loved one has come through that same medium and disguised his energy, and she later stated that he had camouflaged his typical energy and she was unable to identify or recognize him.

What is energy? It is force, or potential force able to move molecules or objects, and comes in the form of heat energy, radiant energy, kinetic energy. The motions of atoms and particles, the reactions of chemicals in cells, the movement of objects or mass are all displays of energy. Energy can express itself in waves and vibrations.

Perhaps we each have a different wavelength or personal vibration. They say thoughts are energy with the power to impress the environment, as in residual feelings or auditory or visual phenomena at a murder scene can be picked up by those who are sensitive, in the environment.

We each carry a unique energy that, for lack of a better word, can be sensed or received by an "attuned" soul receiving it, like we receive sound vibrations that identify a particular note or key with our eardrums.

My guide states, "We know each other by our thoughts, ideas and emotions – the total composite that we are – the mental, "spiritual" part of ourselves. We recognize our core, our energy field we project, that is the result of our thoughts, and feelings, which are the impetus for our deeds and actions. We create with our force. So our force is original, unique to ourselves."

We have magnetic card readers on earth that identify a particular magnetic strip that links the card with a particular bank account. We also each have a unique electromagnetic field or emanation produced by our individual thoughts, ideas, emotions, words, and actions. Each of these carries our "stamp".

We are unique, controlling and intelligent consciousness, that embodies all of our thoughts, emotions, and deeds. We are able to assess/access that unique consciousness which is available to us and registered or received by other spirits. Call it a vibrational or magnetic signature, that other souls can recognize and interpret.

Like the visual receptor cells, the auditory receiving mechanism, the touch sensors that all connect with nerves that transmit electrical signals to the brain, which interprets them and translates them into images, thoughts, and feelings, we, as souls, have a receptor transceiver in our consciousness that is sensitive to incoming vibrations/frequencies, energy waves, and translates them into the recognition of another soul, almost like voice recognition software or a polygraph test.

Our consciousness is like an instrument that receives and interprets electromagnetic information, including that peculiar to another individual soul, and it is that with which we identify them.

Do we have a particular ideogram, pictogram, or sound that we use to call or connect with another individual soul in the afterlife?

It is like a frequency code that is theirs individually that we can attune to in order to contact them or receive if we are contacted by them. It is like a transponder and we are made aware of them, can communicate with them, call or receive calls from them. We can project our individual identifying electromagnetic "sequence or code" to others, or receive theirs, as each is unique. It is like a name that can be translated into sound or symbols as can the earthly equivalent of a written or spoken name.

* * *

If spirits do not have a set appearance, and do not have names, how do we recognize each other in the afterlife?

Harvey's guides:

They will be on the same vibration. On the earth it is called sympathetic resonance. It will not be necessary to recognize another soul by sight. We will recognize them by feelings.

There can be a name but not necessarily. Any of the above is possible. Spirits can maintain a name or appearance if they wish, or they can be recognized by their feelings. There is no scenario that can't be reproduced.

70

Reincarnation Choices

When we are in the afterlife planning our next incarnation, do we have unlimited choice of the birthparents and locations, or are our choices limited by the needs for mutual beneficial lessons for our soul group, and subject to the recommendations of senior spirit advisers?

My guide:

We are given choices based upon what we need to learn, who we incarnate with, and why we need to incarnate. Our choices are modified to provide us the learning opportunities we need and desire. We are always given guidance that will help us accomplish our objectives.

When we cross over and are preparing for another incarnation, do we have unlimited choices, or do we have senior advisers and guides who give us a few choices?

My guide has told me that we have a limited number of options, first because of the billions of souls on the earth. We can't look at all of them before we decide who we want our parents to be and where we want to be born. The choices would be mind-boggling. What if multiple spirits all wanted the same body or birth? The sheer magnitude of choices and complexity would be paralyzing.

Second, if we reincarnate in a soul group, we must all agree to a locale and the interactions so that we all grow, profit, and benefit from the experience. And depending upon what we want to learn, that is, what lessons our soul needs to learn, that shapes and limits our choices so that they are appropriate to our goals.

So the answer I am given is, yes, we have free will, and yes, we have many opportunities, but for a given incarnation, those opportunities are governed by the lessons we want to learn, coordinating the learning situations with our soul group, and controlled by the opportunities available, which are also regulated and mediated by our senior advisers, and teams of elders/guides in spirit. So it is a joint effort melding our free will, choices, and availabilities at that time.

71

Negative Past Relationships

Don't be poisoned by past negative experiences

When someone injures you deeply, and especially if the harmful experiences are repetitive, you can become poisoned and on guard.

This is a bad thing to do because then the person who harmed you has robbed you twice. Once when their actions injured you, and caused you pain, and again when they robbed you of the beautiful gift you have, which is compassion for others.

What happens to people who have had a very injurious or difficult relationship on earth when they get to the afterlife? Maybe one deliberately, intentionally harmed the other.

They examine their lives, find out what they were supposed to learn from each other, make peace, forgive, and go their separate ways. They learn from the experience, bear no animosity, and move on.

When people have had a very happy, loving relationship, they may choose to remain together, but they don't have to. Otherwise we would always be with a wife or husband from one lifetime. As we have had wives and husbands from different lifetimes, we thank one another for the learning and choose who we wish to remain with – if we prefer to remain as a pair or couple – the one we love most deeply.

* * *

What happens to difficult relationships in the afterlife? Do we love all souls equally and spend equal amounts of time with all souls, or do we have individual bonds and loves that are stronger and closer on the other side as we do on earth?

Harvey's guides:

Absolutely. We have closer relationships and loves with some souls than with others, as we did on earth. People who hurt you, you don't automatically love them. We gravitate away from those who hurt us. We don't have to hate them, but we don't have to love them in a personal sense either.

72

Relationships

BAD RELATIONSHIPS

If you are with someone who is taking advantage of you, is unwilling to invest in the relationship or make a commitment, is unwilling to compromise or discuss issues, who defers the responsibility to you rather than sharing it, makes derisive and abusive comments, makes empty promises, lies, hides their past, is sloppy and inconsiderate, you have a selfish, domineering, user, who doesn't truly care for you or your welfare.

Remember, the thief isn't going to ring your doorbell and say let me in so I can rob you and steal everything you have. The suitor isn't going to come to you, curse you and tell you to pay for everything and take on all the responsibility while you are being verbally abused. If you see warning signs such as these, you'd better run in the other direction before the water rises.

What I have learned from my own mistakes and prior unhappy relationships is, "don't take plug nickels." Having someone who doesn't love you is the same as having nothing. In fact, you have something worse than nothing if you have someone who isn't concerned for you or your welfare, someone who will use or harm you.

* * *

Balanced Relationships

A friend and I were discussing the subject of love. The question came up of whether or not people should allow themselves to be used by that person when they love someone.

One friend said that if the abuser is a wife or husband the answer is no but that if the abuser is one's children the answer is yes. I said well, on the other side, all of us are just souls acting in different relationships to those around us each time we reincarnate on the earth. All souls are the same, so why should there be such a distinction?

Besides, are you doing your children a favor by making them perpetual dependents, never requiring or helping them to become independent or autonomous? If they are never able to handle responsibility for themselves, what happens to them when you die?

My friend said that to her there is no love more important than that of a mother for a child. I have heard other people say that the union between a husband and wife is the deepest and that, when it is good, it dominates all others. Children, when grown leave and form their own families. The husband and wife, if they have a good marriage, remain together as companions. The Bible states that one should leave parents and cleave to husband or wife, and the two in essence become one. Certainly, there can be a love for all, a love for children and a love for husband or wife and others.

There are many loves, all valid, different in their essence due to the difference of the relationship and expectations. It does not mean that one is right and another wrong or that one is always more important than another. It just means that they are different depending upon the role, relationship, individual values, and personal affinity between the two. It seems that there are a vast variety of opinions on the subject. So here is mine.

I feel that you can love someone unconditionally without allowing them to belittle, exploit, and use you. It is good to love someone unconditionally, that is, to love them even with their flaws and negative behavior, but not to allow that negative behavior to destroy you or deplete you in such a manner that you are harmed by it.

There should be a balance in which one person should demonstrate respect, caring, loving, and giving towards others, but is also entitled to respect, themselves, and to be happy. If one is always concerned for the happiness of others at the expense of their own happiness, then they are being short changed. Each of us is entitled to decent treatment, dignity, self-respect, and happiness.

There should always be a give and take in relationships. There should be a balance or harmony. Not only should we treat others well, we ourselves deserve to be treated well. Should one person's happiness always be gained at the expense of another? Should one person do all the giving, and the other all the taking, or should one person perform all the sacrifice, and the other reap all the benefits? Isn't each of us entitled to some happiness?

Even the Bible says that God reprimands those he loves. He chastises those of us who are wrong in our behavior in order that we might learn lessons and improve ourselves and our lives. If a child is never corrected in wrongdoing, how can it learn better behavior or benefit from lessons? If a child were indulged by its parents with everything it wanted from the moment it was born to the moment it dies, how could it ever learn independence, growth, or the ability to support itself and make a living?

A book that I read by Shanna Spalding St. Clair channeled an author from Spirit stating that we should be thankful even for tragedy and our most painful life events, because these are what teach us the greatest lessons, how to overcome obstacles and to attempt to find something positive even in negative circumstances, or to address negative circumstances in as positive a manner as possible.

Another friend who is a medium, channeling information from spirit for me, had a similar statement. She said that our most painful experiences on earth are the ones we learn most from. That makes sense, because it is always easy to live if everything is going our way and it is always easy to accept positive circumstances, but the ones that are negative and challenge us are the ones that help us to learn and grow.

It is easy for anyone to experience the positive, but difficult for most of us to overcome the negative. I had a relative whose first marriage ended in divorce, and he was asked, what if the children don't approve of you having a second wife? He answered, I stayed in a very negative marriage until my children were all grown to assure that they could be independent and take care of themselves. I do not owe it to them to remain in an unhappy situation the rest of my life to please them. If I told them who they should marry they would not do it. Why should I? If they really cared about me, they would want me to be happy, not to live according to their own selfish demands and be miserable, myself.

I remember reading in my psychology class long ago that anyone who does not protest against negative behavior in children or in others, is silently endorsing it. In other words, no one is persuaded to desist from a negative behavior if the rewards of the behavior outweigh the punishments. If someone is doing something that is negative toward others, why should they stop if they are never made to suffer the consequences of their behavior?

In the same vein, should someone lie down and be bullied or allow themselves to be attacked or harmed without attempting to stop the aggressor? Should someone allow themselves to be domineered, exploited, or harmed without defending themselves? Aren't we all entitled to decent treatment and respect as human beings? Should one be a doormat for another?

My opinion is that we should not seek to harm others, but, in addition, we should not allow others to harm us. Just as they are entitled to decent treatment, so are we. One person should not have to live in entire self sacrifice to another's happiness.

This does not mean that we shouldn't help others or love others, but that our help and our love do not preclude the expectation of decent treatment for ourselves or the fact that we, too, deserve personal happiness. This doesn't mean that we should never sacrifice for others, for many of us do, but it means that we should not sacrifice to the point of total disregard for our own well-being and happiness. If we do so, we are not helping others to learn to be responsible for their actions or to have concern for someone besides themselves. If we always indulge another person's desires to the disregard of our own, we are doing a disservice to our own selves and neglecting our own needs.

You may choose to live a life of complete self sacrifice for someone else's welfare, but are you really helping them if they never learn to take responsibility for themselves or their actions? Are you helping them if you make them a perpetual dependent or bow continually to the needs of others who are selfish and never learn to have any concern for your own?

In my view, each should learn to give and take, to help others in need, but also to respect their own needs. One should not be entirely subservient to another. To simply indulge another's selfish and inconsiderate behavior is not to help them or ourselves. To help wisely, to preserve our own dignity, to have concern for both ourselves and others, to seek to help others fulfill their potential, but also to fulfill our own, this is mutual love, benefit, and understanding. This promotes the welfare of all concerned. This respects the dignity and well-being of each person. With no boundaries, there is depletion of oneself, and how can one help others or themselves if they are exhausted and drained? Caring for oneself and others is important. There is room for both our own fulfillment, and that of others, for our own measure of happiness, and that of others.

* * *

Ideal Relationships

I was reading some relationship advice online recently and decided to determine some of my own and came up with the following. These are some of the elements in my idea of an ideal partnership.

1. Run to the door, hug, and greet him.
   Keep excitement and enthusiasm alive. It takes two. If one is always the giver and it is never returned, they eventually get tired of the lack of response. If you truly love someone and feel fortunate to be with them, you should be as

excited and expressive the 100 millionth day of the relationship as you were on the first.

2. Don't go to bed angry.
   Always talk things out. Discuss things in a reasonable fashion and be willing to compromise. It goes both ways. Solve your issues, or if they are not solved, they will build an impassable wall of division between the two of you which can no longer be bridged.

3. Never get tired of kissing and embracing.
   Always be willing to show affection and appreciation, even if you're tired or busy. Nothing is more important than your partner. Kissing and hugging, sharing affection and conversation, are the glue that binds a relationship together.

4. Enjoy sex.
   If you can't please your partner or aren't madly attracted to him, you are missing a huge part of the relationship, which includes both emotional and physical intimacy. If you don't desire physical intimacy with your partner, to both give and receive, you have lost a major part of the reason for being in a relationship, and needs are going unmet.

5. Discuss things.
   Be open to discussion. When the channels of communication are closed, you can't fix things or share ideas and concerns. When you have no conversation that involves anything meaningful, you have no relationship

at all, or a bad relationship. It requires communication to fix things and to promote harmony, satisfaction, and understanding.

6. Support each other.
Be glad in your partner's victories and support him in his disappointments. If he can't turn to you for help and support or for appreciation and feelings of accomplishment – triumphs or defeats, who can he turn to? If you are one, as you should be, his accomplishments and defeats are also yours.

7. Loosen up.
Be able to have fun together. Share not only the serious issues, but the silly enjoyments. Be happy together, making memorable good times, even if they're goofy, and enjoy interests, hobbies, and plain old jokes together. Your partner is someone to share both the good times and bad times with. What good is fun if you can't share it with someone, especially the person who is closest to you?

8. Go the extra mile.
If you love someone, give of yourself. Be with them if they are in the hospital, do kind things for them, be solicitous, know how they like a special dinner. Go out-of-the-way to plan a surprise, give a foot rub, or do something special for them. Their happiness is yours and yours is theirs when you are bonded together. As you like to receive special treatment, so do they.

9. Love them for better or worse.
   Let them know you will stand by them, no matter what happens, that you love them for who they are in good times or bad times. Isn't that what you would do if you plan to spend eternity together? You love them regardless of the circumstances, for who they are inside. That kind of love never ends.

10. Learn to forgive.
    You aren't perfect. They aren't perfect. Any happy relationship includes forgiveness. We all inadvertently hurt each other. If you can't overlook the small details, you'll never have a happy relationship with anyone. What matters more? The person you love or some small trifling detail. Be flexible. Do unto others as you would hope they do unto you.

11. Compromise.
    Be flexible. If you didn't marry yourself or aren't in love with yourself, every individual is different. Each must give to have a happy relationship together. Unless your partner is a robot, you will not have a partner who agrees with you on everything. Do you really want a robot? Be open and willing to change if the love is worth it.

12. Be open.
    Don't lie and cheat. If you do, you don't even really know the partner you're with or they you. A relationship based on false premises is no relationship at all, or a bad relationship. If they love the person they think you are, and

that's just an imaginary person in their mind, because there is deception in the relationship, they don't love you. They love who they think you are, not the real you. In other words, if there is deception in a relationship, you love some imaginary person in your mind who doesn't exist, not the person standing in front of you. You can't love someone you don't even know.

13. Treasure private details.
    Have personal details, remembrances, jokes, and memories – things that are uniquely yours – that the two of you alone share together. Have an intimacy that is special to the two of you. Isn't that what a relationship is? About physical and mental closeness? To be one of a kind, the relationship needs to have an intimacy that is not shared with others – otherwise there is no special or exclusive union.

14. Talk and be affectionate.
    Communication involves both mental and physical aspects, and to be complete, must be fostered in both areas. If either of these is missing, the relationship isn't full. It's missing the essentials, if someone should have to look elsewhere for mental or physical fulfillment. Your partner should be your all in all and your closest companion.

15. Concentrate on the positive.
    Unless you live in heaven or paradise, you will encounter negative people and circumstances. Learn how to deal with them without letting them poison you and destroy

the best thing you have, your relationship. We live in a checkered world, with both the good and bad, and facing the difficult times together while remaining positive about each other is one of the best benefits of a good relationship.

16. Don't worry or fear.
    Worry and fear are almost impossible to totally avoid but should be minimized. Take action to optimize a situation as much as you can, do your best, and don't let worry or fear consume you or dictate your life. Worry and fear alone do not accomplish anything. They merely serve as a catalyst to make you take positive action. You should not be paralyzed by either of them, as they can be like quicksand and inhibit forward progression.

17. Be thankful.
    Realize how rare and special your relationship is, and how meaningful it is to you. Be thankful for the special love you give and receive – and if it truly is special, nothing else can replace it. If it is true, recognize it, acknowledge it, and cherish it as a most beautiful gift.

18. Find the right person.
    First of all, find the right person – one with whom you have both mental, spiritual, emotional, and physical compatibility. One with whom you have affinity and harmony. Be sure it is someone who will receive and give love, and that your ideas of love and what you both expect and want in a relationship are similar. If you haven't found the right one (who is not the perfect one, for he doesn't

exist), disregard all the above and wait until you find him. And when you do, and he feels the same way, hopefully you will make that mutual commitment that is reflected in the words of the South Pacific song, Some Enchanted Evening. "Once you have found her (him), never let her (him) go." Realize that that unending true love will probably be the best thing that has ever happened to you. And let your partner know it.

Words from South Pacific's Some Enchanted Evening, say it all.

Some enchanted evening

When you find your true love,

When you feel her call you

Across a crowded room,

Then fly to her side,

And make her your own

Or all through your life you

May dream all alone.

Once you have found her,

Never let her go.

Once you have found her,

Never let her go!

No relationship is ideal because we are not perfect, but if two souls are compatible, love, accept, discuss issues, compromise, forgive, help, support, and appreciate one another, I believe a love relationship like that can be eternal.

A spirit who had been a schoolteacher in her earth life comments in Charlotte Dresser's book, "Life Here and Hereafter", " We see many who come here who have thought they made an alliance that would last forever, who had no real conception of such happiness. It is felt only once by anyone, and can never be mistaken when it really comes. I have watched the growth of several such attractions here, and I realize that the earth life seldom encounters the real thing. Many married people continue together here for a long time, and yet gradually drift apart as they learn the true laws governing such matings....We here know, of course, that it is only a question of temperament and character that determines the depth of the happiness that comes with each mating. But for those concerned, there is never any other that compares with theirs."

Another spirit from the same book channels, "When I first came over, I was thoroughly convinced that there was no marriage in Heaven. Although I saw apparent friendships of more than usual intensity, I did not think of them as inseparable. If I had been communicating with earth at that time, I would have conscientiously said that there was no mating here that was lasting. But now I know that some are drawn together here sometimes by indissoluble ties."

Do all spirits love one another?

Several visiting spirits in a recent Spirit Circle brought home a similar point. They were both here for a woman who was a houseguest of my medium friend, L. I brought through her guest's biological father and Harvey brought through her stepfather. She was astounded, and said they hated each other in life. How was it possible they would come through for her together? We were given the understanding that each now respected the love that the other had for her. They had both put aside their differences and come through to support her. It wasn't about them, but her.

Her biological father gave me a beautiful insight. He said, "We each honor the best part of each other." How aptly said.

* * *

Relationship preferences

As long as we remain individuals, there will be room for greater and lesser loves, room for greater and lesser compatibilities.

If we go over to the other side and become one homogeneous clone, all of us identical, all of us the same, then there will be no need for us to learn lessons as individuals. No personal opinions, preferences, or ideas will exist as we will all be one identical individual without any diversity or any individual consciousness. If individuality and separate consciousness do exist on the other side as I have been told and witnessed in readings given and received, then individual beliefs, preferences, and compatibilities will also exist as on earth.

Certainly there will be more tolerance, understanding, and forgiveness, and a greater concern for all souls in their progress. However, individual compatibilities in relationships will persist, with certain souls closer to one another with greater ties and bonds of love than with others. Although romantic love has been described as an earthly notion, those of us who have lived on earth and have felt it may desire such a relationship if we wish. This may be especially so for those of us who desired it and missed it. As our Creator made it possible and blessed it, it certainly cannot be regarded as wrong or evil. If it isn't important to some souls, neither are other interests and desires, or pursuits important to everyone, as what is important to one of us in life is not necessarily important to another. There is room for various desires, values, and personal choices, both on this side and the other side.

I am told that on the other side we maintain and always maintain free will within the framework of an environment where we are not permitted to harm other souls. If we remain individuals, then we must have certain relationships that are deeper and more aligned, more harmonious, more deeply loving and compatible than others.

We don't know all souls on the other side, as I have been told that some souls met up with each other in the afterlife. Some are souls we have shared this incarnation or other incarnations with, or have known from the other side. However, since we are all individuals with different aspirations, ideas, likes and dislikes, and personal choices, we must have others who are more kindred to us or closer to us in harmony and affinity. We certainly have those who were closer to us and our personalities on earth, so why not on the other side? Even though we are probably more considerate and caring, that doesn't mean we don't have room for special relationships and deeper ties of love.

Think about it. Do we get along with everyone equally on the earth? Do we have the same mind set or affinity with all other souls? We have much deeper bonds with certain friends, certain relatives, and certain loved ones than we do with others because of our individual nature. As we remain individuals with free will, this would persist on the other side.

There are some souls with whom we are completely incompatible. There are some souls in negative relationships. Even though we may iron out differences on the other side, make peace with others, and treat each other better, with more kindness and compassion, that doesn't mean we still don't have differences and prefer to be with some souls more than others.

I think that is why many of the books on the afterlife state that the afterlife is vast with room for many different ideals, opinions, desires, and lifestyles. I have read that we are attracted to those who are of like affinity and that we go to a place that is in accord with our own personal desires and those who are similar to us. We are drawn to conditions that match our personal desires, and other books state that we create our own reality, sometimes a consensus reality, with other souls who have the same desires. This would make sense, as on earth we select our environments that suit us and share our lives with souls who have similar, preferences, ideals, religions, cultures, and affinities. If we seek out environments that are suitable to us on earth, why not also on the other side? We can't live with all souls and spend equal amounts of time with all souls in all different environments, so we obviously select those that are most in harmony with our desires and our individual personalities.

* * *

Soulmate relationships

A medium, Rebecca Rosen, from the TV show, "The Last Goodbye", comments on soulmates that soulmates aren't only romantic relationships but can be parents or siblings as well. Often they are souls that have travelled together before and will be together again many times.

A spirit in Charlotte Dresser's book, "Life Here and Hereafter", when asked if she remains with her earth family, states that it is only ties of congeniality that persist, and that biological earthly relationships endure only if there is soul congeniality.

A friend of mine who is an outstanding medium, D., recently spoke of earthly family ties, and said that sometimes our physical family and soul family are different – that in any given incarnation we choose our physical family through which we enter the earth plane, as well as the interactions we have to learn lessons, but if there is no true lasting inner compatibility, when those lessons are learned, we may part and continue on our own separate individual paths.

What I have learned from unharmonious relationships

1) You can't fix a contentious or inharmonious relationship unless both parties are willing to compromise or change.
2) If the other party is inconsiderate or abusive and is unwilling to change you have 3 options, all with consequences. One is to leave, another to suffer silently, and another to fight.

3) If the welfare of others is at stake you may choose to stay but then should not destroy other people's lives in the process. If you choose to sacrifice your own happiness and subjugate it to the selfishness and happiness of your partner you should not harm others in the process.
4) All of the alternatives are imperfect and have consequences once you have made a bad decision, and carry repercussions. Whatever you decide, you should attempt to do the least harm to yourself and others. It will involve concessions all around.
5) It can be difficult to not get yourself into a bad relationship as not all people are scrupulous and some are deceptive. You can try to discern character but not all things are known about a person and some come out later when pressure or responsibility arrive and the honeymoon or best behavior wear off. Not all problems are avoidable and no one is perfect so look for a good natured, non-abusive person who appears willing to compromise, is considerate, giving, and genuinely appears to care for you and your welfare. Looking for someone with a compatible personality, outlook, and interests will help. Be reasonable in expectations. Remember that you're not perfect. Neither are they. We are all works in progress. Be the person you hope for your partner to be and treat them the way you would like to be treated.
6) If you do get into a difficult relationship and can't fix it, try to resolve it in the best way possible with regard for all involved parties.
7) For me a loving happy compatible relationship is the greatest gift I could ever have and I treasure and am thankful for it unceasingly.

73

Selfishness

SELFISHNESS IS NOT love. It is self gratification. Selfishness acts for the benefit of the self and love for the benefit of the other.

But perhaps I should say selfishness does not really act for the benefit but rather the appeasement of the self, for the soul of a person never benefits from selfishness, but rather lessens instead of broadening.

Love does not seek self gratification at the expense of others or disregard their welfare.

74

Sex

I HAVE BEEN TOLD by one I love on the other side that sex is possible, but merging is better.

We can create or assume a form similar to the physical body if we wish. We can recreate the sensations of touch and sex if we wish. It will be similar to, but not identical to the sex we have on earth. We can re-create the experience. We do not have the biological drives we had on earth but we can have a deep psychological desire for sex.

If the desire is based upon a physical need it will not remain. If it is based on a mental need, it will remain.

We can assume a bodily form and recreate the sensations of sex and touch. It will be similar in terms of how it is perceived. It will feel authentic to those experiencing it.

75

Spirit Sight

C<small>AN SPIRIT SEE</small> us, and is it as it was when they were alive, or as it is now?

My guide:

Spirit can see a place on earth as it is currently, either as it looks now, or as it looked before when they were alive.

They can see us and the objects about us. They can hear us. They can access our thoughts and feelings. They can impress our minds with their thoughts and feelings. They can give us ideas and thoughts, or even actual words. They can impress us with emotions and sensations or feelings.

Do spirits see things on the earth as they are or as they were when they were alive?

Harvey's guides:

They have infinite vision. They can see it as it appeared 100 years ago or today. They can actually make a comparison.

When a soul is near the earth or at a specific earth location, do they see that location as it is presently, or as it was at the time they inhabited it?

John Edward can bring through spirits who demonstrate that they know what is going on in the lives of their loved ones by telling John how their relative's new house looks, what they have, what they are doing, and where rooms are. This demonstrates that spirits can "see" a location as it now looks.

Some psychics and mediums also say that spirits will see a location as it looked to them when they were alive, as they may walk through a wall where a door used to be.

As ghosts can open doors, move items, and interact with the environment, it is clear that they can see things in the present tense. One man on the television show, "Project Afterlife", describes how after he died in the hospital he was walking down the hall and saw some doctors talking and wasn't aware he was "dead" until they didn't move and he walked right through them.

Many cases of haunting indicate that spirits can be upset and become more active after a home renovation. This would suggest that spirits can see the current environment around them if they can be disturbed at the new owner's changes.

I have read that we create our own environment and reality in the afterlife. I had a dream in which my guides showed me an image of myself in the dark night and I heard the words, "She lay there in the dark quietly deciding what she wanted to see." My guides were communicating to me in the third person, indicating that we have the choice or option of our afterlife conditions and environment.

In Jeffrey Marks book, "The Afterlife Interviews", some spirits state that two souls can be together, interacting, and both see things differently, that is, be together, but see their environment differently, or also can agree to a common shared perception.

76

Spirit Sightings By Humans

When spirits are seen by humans and some children on the earth plane, are they seen outwardly in a spirit form by lowering their vibrations, seen clairvoyantly, or both?

Because of their greater clairvoyant gift, those who see spirits are seeing a portion of the spectrum of light and vibration that ordinary people cannot see. They are sensitive to it, receivers, tuned differently.

The degree of their receptivity or gift determines how solid spirits will appear to them and this can also be enhanced by the spirits' energy and ability to manipulate or lower their vibration.

There is no single answer. We can see spirits both outwardly and clairvoyantly, depending on the situation and the spirit's energy and ability to lower their vibration and manifest themselves.

Can spirits manifest in a "solid" touchable form to help people?

Harvey's guides:

There have been many, many occurrences of people who have been helped and the people who help them were untraceable. There is no reason that they couldn't.

Spirits do it all the time. They can be seen and felt- a longer emanation that's possible. Many cases have been reported of so-called angels.

There are many reported cases of people being helped by someone who inexplicably disappears minutes later, or someone who sees a person or place and returns to find it gone. There are children who saw "people" that came to them when they were in distress, but no one else could see these helpers.

I, myself, know of a man who had a drug addiction and walked into a park with the intention of ending his life, only to find himself joined on a park bench by a person who talked him out of suicide and then, when he turned around to thank the man seconds later, found that he had vanished into thin air.

How is it that some spirits remain on earth, sometimes a hundred or more years after their death, often in cases where they were murdered or had a horrible life or death? Don't they recognize the passage of time, and why don't they prefer to go to the light?

My guide:

It can be because they are confused, but is most often because they feel they are not strong enough. Although some may fear retribution for their misdeeds, or be attached to a place or person they loved, some who have been emotionally traumatized have issues, unresolved business or conflicts. They are paralyzed by the emotion, which makes them incapable of moving forward.

That is why some mediums can talk to them and convince them to transition. They may need the equivalent of earthly counseling. When the normal routines and the needs of a physical body are gone, they are not as sensitive to the passage of time. They lose track of time. The passage of time is no longer "real" or relevant to them. Imagine, if you didn't have the cycles of night and day or seasons, the routines of work and sleep, or the demarcations of calendars, would you be able to assess how much time had passed, or even how old you were?

77

Trance Channeling

On a recent radio show of medium, L., Matthew Smith, a tutor from the Arthur Findlay College of mediumship in England, went into trance and publicly answered questions submitted by the radio audience, many of which were from me.
He channeled:

"You have the key to a closer understanding of life, purpose, and destiny. There is an ever open door. God loves us. We are our own judge and jury. Never underestimate the power of compassion. We can't be alone. The key is the spiritual power of self. Allow spirit to walk through. When your mind becomes more dominant, spirit withdraws. Spiritualism is the key of life. Our purpose is to utilize the gifts we've been given. Because we have free will, we have free will about how our destiny is weaved.

Always look for recurring situations. When there are recurring negative situations in our lives, we haven't listened to the spirit within. Without free will we wouldn't learn through mistakes and the lessons that come with them. We are on the path that we are meant to be on.

Keep a clear open mind if you are investigating spiritual matters. You don't have to accept anything that is written in any book or anything that any other person says to you. If it doesn't fit right for you, then it isn't for you. As Gordon Higginson, the trance medium said, "It's not what is said, it's how it makes you feel." We have free will on how our destiny will weave its way. The key is your spirit. The door is your life.

When we die the spirit is reborn. That individual essence or the life force within will continue and progress into a place it has created through the life which he or she has lived. You make the world in which you live. We will be reunited with those we have loved. We will never be reunited with those we haven't, because love is the answer. Love is the essence of all life. We are light of varying energy.

Daily we meet with people we can and cannot connect with. In this life we cannot love everyone, but we can try to understand them."

* * *

What is the afterlife environment like?

"It is a world which is not far away. There is no night or day. We are surrounded with perpetual love. The soul is the life force. It goes to a place it has created by its thoughts, words, and deeds. Always remember, you clothe your body. What do you do for your spirit? Each one of us has a guide. There are no dogmas or creeds in the afterlife. The universal law is compassion towards one another. Give a sense of hope and encouragement to those who have lost their way."

* * *

Is there such a thing as a specific God-given intent for each of us?

"There is a destiny for each of us. Each of us is born with a plan, and within that plan, there are lessons for that individual to learn, and when the individual finds the reason for their existence, life does not become a battle. It becomes a way of life. Embrace who you are. Then you will feel the purpose of your own life.

Our essence chose its pathway and its destiny. We have chosen to learn certain lessons – it may be tolerance, forgiveness, many different things. When those lessons have been learned, more lessons will come along that are required for that soul's progression. Anything that harms another is not in destiny. God has not created wars or famine. The power an individual thinks he has over another, those things, including greed and avarice, originate from the darker human mind. Life is for the purpose of giving understanding."

* * *

What is the afterlife environment like?

"There are realms of similarity where people feel comfortable, but only if it is required.

Buildings, nature, appearances, and activity are similar but there is no experience of time or space in the sense that we know it on earth. We gravitate to places that are familiar to us and that hold memories for us. There is an etheric world which is very similar to that of the earth, where memories have been stored from the individual's physical existence. Souls can spend time there until they adjust or become accustomed to the next phase of life. It is like going home. When the individual has progressed, then they are ready to move. Then the individual concerned progresses into atmospheres and places that are not the same, because they are ready to take the next step along their pathway."

* * *

Do we maintain our individual identities when we reunite with Source?

"Humankind can only assimilate themselves as the personality they are now, but in truth, you and those listening are an expression of their spirit. If God is a diamond, you are a facet. The personality, the individual you has been created, perhaps from a genetic aspect and also from lifestyle, and when you come into the next stage of being, the power that is you will remain for as long as you need it to, and then eventually you will return to that source, that higher power. In the same manner, an animal sheds it's skin. Don't think of yourselves as who you are now, but as where you have come from, and where you will return. You were born to be who you are. Aspects of the personality are required to function in physical form. When the spirit is reborn, all that will be retained is all that is necessary for the soul's progression."

✳ ✳ ✳

Can we fulfill dreams on the other side that we never had the chance to realize when on earth?

"This will vary according to the needs of the individual. There are aspects in our world that cannot be compared with that of the earth, and equally, the same can be said with us. The opportunities present themselves for people to learn their life's lessons, and if those lessons have not been learned, it is possible for an individual to recapture a learning experience on this side of life, of course. The opportunity will be presented to them. But, if not, then it can't. The lifestyle, the structure of life from both sides of existence does differ in some ways. We don't have a competition of learning. We don't have a thrust of one-way being better than the other. These things occur in the physical form because of ignorance."

✳ ✳ ✳

How is the afterlife different from the earth life?

"We are not restricted by a thought of time. We don't have night and day. There is no time in the sense that it's eternity. Death is a great liberator from the restrictions the physical world can bring. You are not restricted in any way by people whose opinions you are taught. The light of who you are is who you are. Some people on earth hide behind masks. When the spirit is reborn, there is no mask to hide behind. See with the eyes of spirit, speak with the voice of your own spirit, and bring that same liberation to others. We do not have a physical body to feed. Our work does not have to be for financial reasons. We don't have to meet material obligations because those things are not necessary. They are necessary for progression of the spirit while in physical form but fall away. Our world is the reality. The physical world is the dream. When you return home, you are fully awake."

* * *

How do spirits transmit information?

"Everything is produced through the power of thought. We are projecting thought, emotion, and feeling to bring information and clarity to help other people. It is a form of telepathy built within the intention of those who wish it to be so."

* * *

How does the spirit world work with writing and trance?

> "They work with the individual level of perception. Many people work with Spirit and are not even aware of it. They are inspired.
>
> If we want someone to be aware of it, we will make them aware of us. Just sit quietly and talk with us.
>
> Photographs and flowers can bring energy and deeper love."

* * *

Does individuality persist in the afterlife?

> "Perceptions remain different. Souls have different opinions in the spirit world also.
>
> Thoughts are living things. They make you who you are. I didn't want to forget who I was.
>
> A thought has just come into my head. Spirit just said to me, "Don't chase rainbows, make them." There's a message in that for someone in the audience. When we look at something and consider why it is bad in our life, we must realize that we have powers in ourselves to change it because we have free will."

* * *

The life review

"You see your life. You are shown it as on a movie screen in your own mind. I saw the distress I caused. The momentary happiness didn't outweigh the harm I caused to others."

* * *

How do you become a guide?

"It didn't happen in a short space. I became a guide over a period of time."

* * *

Love and relationships

"You'll only come over here to those you love." (This implies there are some you don't love)

* * *

What is the spirit appearance like?

"It is a mental impression. They're projecting who they were."

* * *

Albert

"We are more alive than those that say they're living. I was a rag and bone man. I thought when you were dead, you were dead. I had a horse that I loved and lived in the reign of Queen Victoria in England. There were those who had money and those who didn't. I didn't. Times were hard. I used to help myself. It was wrong. It would be called stealing. When I came over here, I had to put it all right. I liked to drink. When I died, I saw my horse and thought what are you doing here? You're dead. And then it occurred to me, so are you. You can't die even if you want to.

I loved my horse. She's still with me, Alice. I do love my horse. I loved her more than my wife. I didn't cry a tear when my wife died. I was happy, really. You are attached to those you love. When my horse, Alice, died, it was terrible. Some people say they have their soulmates. They've got that special bond between them. You don't find that with everybody.

Guides don't have to be super spiritual. We are showing our identity. Some who come over will have a shock. It's how you live your life. I had to put it right. You can't hide your errors when you come into heaven. You have to put it right. That's the natural law. So does everybody else. Everybody would do that in their own way. Smile more.

Comprehend your own consciousness. There is a reason and purpose for why you are where you are. There are different vibrations in the afterlife, different levels. People's perceptions are important. People gravitate to places where they feel comfortable. It's the same in the earth environment. There are people you feel at one with and people you do not. There is no difference in our environment. There are many levels of consciousness, too many to comprehend. Accept where you are rather than trying to be what you are not. Live in the reality of who and where you are.

When you see spirits, they are a manifestation of love. Each person will be different. There are many answers and many different situations, but all are produced through the power of love."

* * *

Why is it that some questions are not clearly answered?

"That is because we can't always put into words our spiritual life. We have to deal with physical comprehension, which often seems black or white. There are more colors in the spectrum. Each person and each spirit sees things according to their own lifestyle and understanding. We leave culture and lifestyle behind us when we come to this world. Who we were is not important. We are freer. You are liberated to be who you are."

* * *

Is everything in our lives predestined?

"Not everyone comes into our world at the appointed time. There are tragedies and accidents. We try to allow them to come back into the same family to reincarnate to fulfill that which he or she was not able to fulfill on their journey. When people go to war, it is not the higher mind of God. It is man's inhumanity to man. Do not be cross with God."

* * *

Is there reincarnation? Are our choices for reincarnation restricted or unlimited?

"Individuals will reincarnate if there is a need in that soul's evolution to experience what is needed within that physical incarnation. Everything is arranged according to the needs required, not just for the person incarnating, but for those in the family or friendship unit. The plan is perfect."

* * *

Learning difficulties

"People who incarnate into the world with learning difficulties or handicaps are teachers. They teach people compassion, tolerance, and understanding. People who are looking on learn from the situation. A soul undertakes that role to convey a deeper understanding to others."

* * *

Lessons

"All lies within the ability of the individual to progress. When you look at things with negativity, it is hard for spirit to speak to you or through you. Don't look at the clouds, look at the sunshine."

Are there other dimensions or worlds into which we incarnate?

"The human mind is limited. There are many other levels of consciousness in the physical chain. Life is needed for progression. When you look through a telescope, there are many other worlds beyond those apprehended by physical sight. There are worlds within worlds."

78

A Song

About Love:
No more shattered hearts
No more broken dreams
No more living life
That isn't what it seems
Now I have the love
That I was looking for
I have the dream I dreamed
And could never ask for more.
I once had a hope I carried in my heart
Of a love that was true, of two who wouldn't part,
Somewhere along the way that hope seemed to die
And all I ever found was disappointment and lies.
I lived the best I could and made so many mistakes,
All the while doing whatever it takes,
And then one day it happened, my heart found you,
I'll never turn back for in my heart I knew,
What I've done wrong, it doesn't matter any more,

PRUDENCE ANN SMITH MD

I've found the one love I was always looking for,
I can move past my mistakes and leave the past behind
With a healed heart and with a new mind.
In our love I have the joy that will never cease
A soul that's fulfilled, a heart that has peace,
Happiness at last, and when all is said and done,
I'll love you forever, and we are one.

MAKING RAINBOWS

About individuality:
I can't live the life you want me to,
I have to find my dream, not one that pleases you,
I have to walk my path by the compass of my soul,
I can't play another actor's role.

Sing your own song, play your own tune,
Write your own script, honor you,
Live your own life, Find your own star,
Make your own dreams come true.

I can't be who you want if I try,
The bed I make's the one in which I'll lie,
If I make mistakes and things fall apart,
At least I'll be true to my own heart.

Sing your own song, play your own tune,
Write your own script, honor you,
Live your own life, Find your own star,
Make your own dreams come true.

79

Current Theories

TWO POINTS IN the current literature on which I disagree

It has been stated that there is no time. That isn't true. We act in the now, cannot change what we did in the past, and plan for the future. If we have free will, which we do, we must be able to change our minds and modify the future. Without the future there is no free will. We can't go back and change the past as we would be changing other people's lives and experiences at the same time.

As we know on the other side we are eternal, don't age, don't have nights and days, months and seasons, and don't sleep daily or eat at meal times, time is not important. It doesn't have the same relevance.

But there is still a past, present, and future.

There is also a reference to multiple simultaneous reincarnational selves. That would lead you to believe we are more than one soul. No. We are the same soul inhabiting different bodies in different circumstances and cultures, and have different experiences.

If Harvey was Matilda in a different lifetime 100 years ago, but they are both simultaneous reincarnational selves, then there could be no progression, because if we are different souls or live simultaneously, we could never learn from our past experiences and mistakes, because there would be none. Harvey could never benefit from or learn from the experiences he had in a different body in a past life if they are two separate souls or in existence simultaneously.

In order to progress we must first have a past, not just simultaneous experiences, and number two, we must be able to learn from the past – our past mistakes, and in order to change we must have a future. Otherwise there would be no need to learn.

So we couldn't progress if we are separate souls living at the same time – in order to progress you must have a past to learn from. If you have choices, learning experiences, and direction, you must have a future.

And if you could go back and change your past, then you would ipso facto be changing the learning experiences of all the souls who interacted with you. So that would not be allowable.

One writer referred to ancient religion as no longer relevant for us because it was only good for the circumstances of the world at that time, and not applicable or relevant to us in our current time. What? If there is no time, how can one say there is a past, it's different from the present, and no longer relevant for us? How can there be an obsolete past or even a past at all if there is no time, and we are multiple simultaneous incarnational selves?

I respectfully disagree.

We are one soul, the same soul, putting on different bodies and learning through different experiences through the course of time, growing from our past experiences, making new choices in the present, and incorporating our previous learning into the decisions we make that shape our future.

80

Spirit Thought Transmission

How do spirits transmit information and visual images or emotions into our minds? What is the mechanism?

My guide:

It is a transmission of energy from spirit to spirit, mind to mind, a coding and decoding of thought, feelings, and images by a directed transmission of vibrational energy, a non-human form of transmission, not interpreted by the human sense organs and brain. It is a different form of reception and reading based upon waves and vibrations at a different frequency and energy level.

81

Trust

THE QUESTION OF trust is a difficult one. It is said that it is good to trust, but how can you trust if you have been repeatedly lied to and your trust has been repeatedly abused and undermined by people throughout your lifetime?

The conclusion I have reached is that trust needs to be tempered by wisdom and judgment. You need to trust cautiously, not blindly. You need to assess and judge the character of someone that you potentially trust, not just their words, but their actions also.

It is said in the Bible that we are to trust God, a good and loving God, and it also says is God a man that he should also lie? Of course not. Men are trustworthy in proportion to their godliness. Godliness does not mean church attendance or ritualistic observations. Godliness means inner integrity, charity and goodness. Godliness means adherence to moral values and the conviction not to harm others.

So trust is important, as what kind of world would we live in if we never could trust anyone? Would that be a world worth living in? Would a world without love be worth living in to you? It wouldn't to me. But trust, like love, is not always what we think it is, and the word can be travestied.

Therefore, when we either trust or love, we need to evaluate whether this truly is love and whether someone or something warrants our trust. Evaluate the situation, the relationship, what the other individual says and does. Then decide whether that person truly loves you and merits your trust. While you are assessing others, turn your eye inward and assess yourself. Also determine whether you truly love others and whether you merit their trust.

82

Seeking The Truth

THE TRUTH IS in you. The spirit is in you. When you seek it, you'll find it, when you listen to it, you'll hear it.

How? Meditate on your life, trust, and it will be given to you by spirit, both your own, and those on the other side, by God or Source if you ask for it. Enlightenment will be given by a loving God who is able to spiritually impart wisdom and love to those who seek him or his spirit. As the Bible said, as earthly fathers are able to give good gifts to their children, so much more is our heavenly father, whose spirit is in us, able to give good gifts to his children.

We can receive those inner gifts of hope, knowledge, peace, joy, and love in the spirit – not as the world gives – like a Cadillac or a bank account. This is a spiritual bank account, filled with love, hope, and greater understanding – the treasure that moth does not eat and rust does not corrupt. These are concepts from the Bible, but fleshed out in the way they have played out in my life, not in a prideful way, but in a humble way.

It's receiving the wisdom and then learning to apply it, working and moving, as all creation, toward greater perfection. We are all learning from each other and from God. It doesn't mean you are sacrosanct or exclusive. It just means, "learn to do better." Who couldn't stand to do better at some point in their life? The only time you fail is when you quit.

I am trying to minimize the lesser parts of myself and ignite the better. It is a process.

I am trying to become less given to the whims of the physical and more shaped by the spiritual principles. I am willing to learn and change, and I desire to learn and change. The more I believe in accord with the spiritual principles, the happier I will be despite the insults of the physical world, for I will have found "myself", the true self, that is worthy to give and receive love.

Part of the learning process is experiencing and imparting my thoughts. Peace is in spirit, not in the world. But it is in us while in the world while we are in spirit. It is the inner peace of knowing the truth and of love. We can know it while in the body. Our spirit knows it.

Am I "holier than thou?" Absolutely not. We all have to find our own answers within. These are the answers I have found on my path forward, improving, stumbling and falling along the way, then getting up and proceeding again. It is only through attempting to understand things that we move forward.

We are all spiritual beings in the same boat. There is no race, color, or gender. We are all of the same spirit material, wearing different uniforms. Sometimes the boat may rock in the storm, but when we realize that we are the pilot and that there is a loving copilot, that is when we have peace. Underneath the shell we are all of the same spirit, individualized by our thoughts, creeds, personality, and beliefs.

I am just a child of God, attempting to do better, as are you, you, you, and all of us in our own way. I desire to help and inspire others along their path as others have inspired and helped me along mine. May you love and be loved.

To my loved one and guide, you are my inspiration, my desire to move forward, and to learn to make myself better. You are the love and light of my soul.

83

Twin Flames

I ASKED MY GUIDE why some books say there are twin flames and some say there are not.

I was told that just like in any walk of life there are some spirits that are more advanced in knowledge than others. There are also personal belief systems which affect our conclusions. In addition, there are different experiences and regions in the afterlife, and what may be one person's experience may not be another's.

He told me that there are such things as twin flames and that we are twin flames.

They are two souls broken off from Source and originating at the same time, who are very similar and designed to be guardians for one another's progress. Other authors refer to twin flames as a soul that has been divided into parts and lives as separate entities until it recombines. Some texts have indicated that twin flames are eventually reunited into one.

Unions are vows of commitment made into the Akashic records by souls who wish to remain together, to not be parted throughout their existence. It is a way of expressing love and an eternal commitment and relationship with one another. There are those who are so bonded. It is a very deep and serious commitment recognized by those of the advanced spiritual dimensions.

84

Veil Between the Worlds

ONE MEDIUM'S ARTICLE I recently read said there really is no veil between the two worlds, physical and spirit. Is there such a veil?

Only a vibrational or frequency veil exists. Otherwise, we could all see and hear spirits. The material world operates on a different frequency and our sensory apparatus is not attuned to receive or recognize the world of spirit.

Since we are souls in bodies, we also have spirit bodies residing in our physical framework, and it is the spirit body that can pierce or transcend the so-called veil. If we can tap into and learn to operate with our spirit "senses" of clairvoyance, clairaudience, clairsentience, and claircognizance, we have pierced the veil. The veil is the frequency shift that prevents our physical sensory mechanism from seeing and hearing the discarnate spirits.

Activating, awakening, and using our spirit perception faculties allows us to override or circumvent, leap that veil, so to speak. So there is a veil, but it is a barrier only to the physical, and when we learn to utilize our spirit faculties, we shortcut or short circuit that veil, and establish contact with spirit.

85

Verbal Abuse

IF SOMEONE HAS a need to belittle or demean another person by calling them derogatory names, they do not care for that person. They are attempting to assert their own superiority by preying upon someone they regard as weaker.

When someone cares about someone else, they lift them up, encourage them, not demean them. Someone who has a need to demean others is trying to bolster their own self-esteem at the expense of others. However, they cannot confirm their own self-esteem, because, in the act of deliberately harming others, they are eroding their self-esteem, not building it. They lack integrity.

Maligning someone else cannot give you integrity.

86

Near Death Visions

IN NEAR DEATH experiences some people see Jesus or hell or other deities. If the afterlife is the product of our imagination and what we expect to see, how can we ever know what the truth is? If that were the case, the afterlife would just be a dream world of hallucination.

My guide:

On earth we know what we perceive and can measure the environment around us. There is a common agreement among observers.

How do we know what is "real" on the other side?

We create our own reality with our thoughts rather than our hands. We can create our own reality or create a reality in concert with other souls who experience the same reality. It's like a kid playing with an erector set. You can create on your own and others can observe your reality or you can create a reality with another group of souls observed by all in the group.

Realities and environment are not as fixed and can be manipulated by thought, but are nevertheless reality. They are more quickly and readily changed and responsive to thought.

Because we create with our thought and do not need hands as we do on earth, just because we create more directly, this does not mean that what we create is not real. Our experience and apprehension of our circumstances is as real to us as the chair and table in your room are to you.

In a near death experience, when someone needs to receive a message, they are sent someone they can connect with to deliver that message, whether a relative, loved one or religious figure.

They are seeing discarnate souls and visions of the afterlife. When they see visions they feel to represent hell, they are seeing a place of unrest where souls are sent who are unable to advance to a higher realm.

You are assigned a place you have "purchased" with your deeds and you may have psychological torment and suffering where you experience the product of your thoughts, and it feels real to you.

When people get to the other side and see Jesus or hell or Krishna, are they really seeing that soul, or is it just a hallucination?

Harvey's guides:

It's not a hallucination. They see the person they have been with through their belief system on earth. There can be lots of figures in their lives through religion and socialization. And when they pass over, there's no reason they can't contact them, and it's very comforting in their transition.

God can be in many places at one time with many visages. He can appear as anything. What people hear can absolutely be the voice of God. Lots of times on the earth plane you hear voices that are very compelling, and because of your teaching, you accept them as God, Buddha, Abraham, Moses, Etc.

Why can't God speak through anyone? And his voice would convey the truth. Yes, we can still hear the voice of God when we are on the other side.

87

Destiny and Free Will

ONE OF MY two favorite authors had a quotation on her web site that stated that what we think, do, and say today is what we become tomorrow. In other words, our thoughts are a catalyst to our future development and identity. What we choose to do, we manifest. What we believe and desire, we become.

88

Words of Comfort

WORDS OF COMFORT/COMMENTS to me from spirit

My dog has recently passed. I was very troubled because my previous dogs had lived such a long time and this dog died comparatively early. I was also upset because I was so overloaded at work, I regretted not having more time to give my dog love and affection.

    Just as I was awakening, one morning, soon after her death, my guide gave me the words, "Holly is in training to be a guardian." My guide and loved one in spirit gave me a scenario through another close friend of mine who is a medium, to comfort me. She saw an image of my loved one dressed up in black tie and tails with a black top hat and a fake mustache dancing and performing, with my dog, Holly, dressed up likewise with a top hat, black-and-white bib, and fake mustache, dancing with him, and he gave me the song I've Got You Babe, which was popular in the 1960s. He also told me that he was caring for her and that I would be able to be with her and take care of her when I transition across to the next phase of life.

Another experience I had while I was relaxed and just awakening was a comment from my guide stating, "She lay quietly in the darkness, deciding what she wanted to see." I feel my guide was describing my state after I die, indicating that our belief system and desires determine who and what we will see, not that we are creating a hallucination, but that, like on earth, when we are sitting at a computer choosing a vacation destination or a hotel, we have choices of what we wish to experience in the afterlife.

89

The Physical World

THE PHYSICAL WORLD isn't all evil. Physicality is not by essence wrong or bad. The physical world permits duality, that is, the exercise of good or evil in the physical by free will and choice.

The purpose of life is not to negate or nullify the physical but to act in accordance with good spiritual principles while in the physical.

In other words, all sensuality is not evil. The enjoyment of sex, the institution of marriage, the procreation of children, the network of family, the pursuit of employment, the acquisition of shelter and material objects necessary to living, the act of eating, the desire of knowledge, these things are not inherently bad.

They are not in and of themselves wrong as they form a part of our physical life and are necessary elements of a physical existence. Physical existence is not of itself wrong or bad. Wrong or bad occurs when we make choices in our physical existence that harm ourselves or others, choices that disrupt harmony, that cause disagreements, that inflict harm. These are choices that result from bad intentions or selfishness.

The Bible states that evil begins in the heart with wrong thoughts, bad intentions, and these are expressed in words and actions, but begin as thoughts, desires, and willful choices.

If marriage were inherently bad, why would God have created marriage? If sex were inherently wrong, why would God have created and permitted sex? If owning material possessions were evil, why would the necessity of some possessions be required for physical maintenance in life?

It is a mistake to say that all things physical are wrong or bad and to be abnegated, denied, and overcome. They are not wrong or bad in and of themselves, but by improper usage. It is the intentions and actions, the thoughts that make wrong, not the institutions and material objects. It is what we do with them.

God said be not unequally yoked together, and that it is a great mystery, but two become one, in a spiritual marriage. God said man was created to need a helpmate. Therefore the institution of marriage and the desire of companionship are not evil. They are good when kindness, love, happiness, completion, concern, and caring, are created and become the fundamental values in the relationship.

When controversy, conflict, disagreements, lack of consideration, selfishness, abuse, exploitation, and discord are at the heart of a relationship, then that marriage or companionship is bad. It is not the thing in and of itself that is bad, but what we do with it.

A gun can be used to defend your life, to defend the lives of those we love, to protect our property from theft and robbery, to protect ourselves and our loved ones from harm, assault, and murder. A gun can also be used to murder, rob, assault, harm, and inflict pain.

All things that we see in the physical are but instruments, tools used and employed by us for good or for evil.

It is my conclusion, therefore, that marriage, sex, having children, owning possessions, choosing a career, eating, all the things that we do in the flesh, are not necessarily wrong. They can be used for right or wrong, for betterment, or misery. Used in a loving manner and employed with good intentions, all of these items, although part and parcel of the gross physical or material environment, can be enjoyed appropriately and with love.

Should a good and loving marriage be condemned because it is an earthly institution? Should sex be regarded as vile when practiced with honor and love between two loving souls? Should eating be regarded as evil when it is necessary for bodily maintenance? Should possessions be regarded as negative if enjoyed without pride or selfishness?

It is obvious that in the spirit world, which is not physical, the same institutions, habits, and objects are likely not necessary. Perhaps there are greater equivalents or finer equivalents to the things we enjoy in the physical. That does not make the physical bad or wrong, only the inappropriate usage, motivation, and handling of the things we encounter in the physical environment.

90

Afterthoughts

Poetic Inspiration

Thoughts on my loved one and guide

Love is eternal.
It fills and completes my soul.
It helps me to endure or overcome the vicissitudes of life.
It gives me a reason to want to be a better person.
It gives me hope in the face of disappointment and grief.
It is the solace, comfort, and strength of my endeavors.
It is the answer to my prayers.
Your love is my dearest wish come true.
You are the best partner I could ever imagine.
My heart swells with pride to know that I have the honor and privilege of sharing life with you, to stand by your side, and know that you love me.
My home is your home.
My love is your love.
I love you eternally.

MAKING RAINBOWS

Bear the sword of righteousness. Speak the word of life. Let us write our future together. I wish to aspire to higher and higher plateaus with you. We reach for beauty the eye does not comprehend, eternities beyond the scope of mortal understanding. Come explore with me.

Though the sands of time shift,
Yet my love stands steady;
Though the winds of time blow change,
Yet my love is sure.
Though the very foundations of existence quake,
Yet my love will not falter.
My love for you is true and knows no end.
You have given me the gift of transformation.
You have opened a door that will never close.

Thoughts on God and life

God is my Source and my strength.
Life is an opportunity for expansion to be explored, not a burden to be borne.
We are human. We mess up. What we do next is what counts.

BIBLIOGRAPHY

Borgia, Anthony, *Life in the World Unseen*, (Kindle Edition, 2009) (Original Work Published 1954)

Cummins, Geraldine, *Beyond Human Personality*, (London, England: Psychic Press, 1935)Marks, Jeffrey A., *The Afterlife Interviews*, Vol. I and II, (Mukitleo, Washington, Arago Press, 2013 and 2014)

Dresser, Charlotte & Rafferty, Fred, *Life Here and Hereafter*, (San Jose, California: Cosmos, 1927)

Dresser, Charlotte & Rafferty, Fred, *Spirit World and Spirit Life*, (Kindle Edition, 2010) (Original Work Published 1922)

Marks, Jeffrey A., *The Afterlife Interviews*, Vol. I and II, (Mukitleo, Washington, Arago Press, 2013 and 2014)

Sandys, Cynthia, *The Awakening Letters*, (Channel Islands, Great Britain, Neville Spearman Limited, 1978)

Sandys, Cynthia, *The Awakening Letters, Vol. II*, (Essex, England, The C. W. Daniel Company Limited, 1986)

Scott, John, *As One Ghost to Another*, (London, England: Spiritualist Press, 1948)

St. Clair, Shanna Spalding, *Karma I and II*, (no location provided: S. C. Walter, 1993)

Wands, Jeffrey A., *Another Door Opens*, (New York, NY, Atria Books, 2006)

Author Biography

Prudence Ann Smith, MD, FACR, is a board-certified practicing physician who has always been fascinated with the mysteries of life and death. On the quest to develop her own mediumship, she has trained with a number of well-known psychic mediums, including Robert Brown, Lisa Williams, and James Van Praagh.

Smith is the author of three books about her life-altering journeys into the spiritual side of life: *The Afterlife: Conversations With My Guide*, *Two Mediums*, and *Making Rainbows*.

www.ingramcontent.com/pod-product-compliance
Lightning Source LLC
LaVergne TN
LVHW051038080426
835508LV00019B/1594